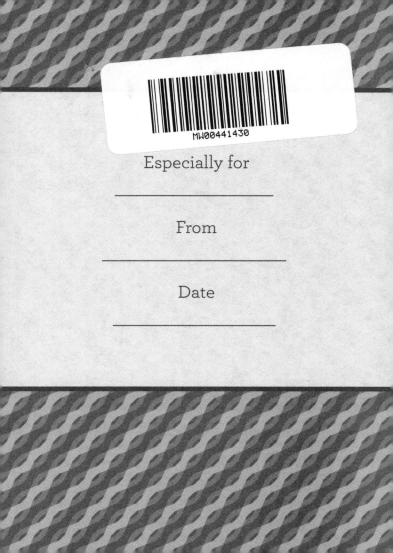

Especially for

_____

From

_____

Date

_____

3-MINUTE DEVOTIONS FOR DADS

Inspiring Devotions and Prayers

BARBOUR
PUBLISHING

© 2014 by Barbour Publishing, Inc.

Print ISBN 978-1-62416-862-8

eBook Editions:
Adobe Digital Edition (.epub) 978-1-62836-998-4
Kindle and MobiPocket Edition (.prc) 978-1-62836-999-1

Writing and compilation by Dwight Clough, in association with Snapdragon Group℠, Tulsa, OK.

Published by Barbour Publishing, Inc., P.O. Box 719, Uhrichsville, Ohio 44683, www.barbourbooks.com

Our mission is to publish and distribute inspirational products offering exceptional value and biblical encouragement to the masses.

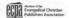
Member of the
Evangelical Christian
Publishers Association

Printed in the United States of America.

INTRODUCTION

Human beings live within a web of connectedness. We are sons to one generation and dads to another, as well as husbands, brothers, uncles, cousins, and grandsons—giving, receiving, being, and doing all in the course of our lifetimes.

No other relationship so easily takes on spiritual significance, however, than that of father to child. Through it we are constantly learning to be better human beings, but we also gain important insights into what it means to be a child of God, to know our Creator as heavenly Father.

These devotions are written especially for men who want to grow as strong, caring fathers to their children, and faithful, understanding sons of faith as well. We pray that when you read these stories, you will see wisdom and find ways to incorporate that wisdom into your own relationships.

Being a dad is a tough job—a lot like walking a high wire without a net—but if you look into the eyes of your children, you'll see that God thought you were up to the task. You even have His perfect example to go by.

See what great love the Father has lavished on us, that we should be called children of God!

1 JOHN 3:1 NIV

ONE OF A KIND

Yes, the body has many
different parts, not just one part.
1 CORINTHIANS 12:14 NLT

Each child is unique. Even children raised by the same parents in the same home are often radically different. We dads discover this in many different ways.

For example, a dad was reading his young daughter the children's storybook *Frosty the Snowman*. Things were going along fine until they got to the part where Frosty melts. Then the tears started flowing. Frosty melted! "It's okay," her dad said. "Frosty will come back." But that didn't comfort her. For days she mourned the loss of this magical snowman. Nothing her dad could say or do would stem her grief. Frosty melted! She was inconsolable.

Clearly this was a dangerous story to share with children, and the father tried to protect his second child, a son, from hearing it. But word leaked out, and the boy exhibited an entirely different reaction: He looked around the room at nothing in particular.

"What?" he said. "Someone melted?"

The third child held up his imaginary flamethrower and smiled. "I bet I could get him to melt a lot faster." The fourth child, another daughter, expressed her thoughts like this: "Serves him right. If he's dumb enough to go dancing around on a warm, sunny day, he deserves to melt!"

No wonder as fathers we find that each child presents unique challenges and opportunities. What works with one child may not work with another. We love all our children equally, of course, but the relationship we have with each is unique.

Likewise, God honors the singularity of each of His children. No cookie-cutter formula works for a relationship with God, because each of His children is one of a kind. We need not fret if our relationship with God doesn't look like someone else's. He relates to each of us as individuals.

Father in heaven, thank You for seeing me as a unique individual and for letting me know that I will never be just a face in the crowd to You. Amen.

THE POWER OF WORDS

"Bless me—me too, my father!"
GENESIS 27:34 NIV

Suppose humans had the power to make something happen just by speaking it. How would we use that power? What would we bring into being? It's easy to imagine all sorts of things, from ending world hunger to conjuring up an enjoyable family vacation.

In fact, our words are powerful, especially in the lives of our children. For example, our words give our children a sense of identity. "You are designed to make a difference. You are beautiful. You are capable." The way we see and define ourselves is critical. It's the foundation our future is built on. If our children believe they have what it takes, they will move through life with confidence and assurance. If they believe they are loved and lovely, they won't feel the need to seek love and affirmation in the wrong ways.

With our words, we help our children imagine a brighter future. We inspire them to go after higher goals and more meaningful achievements by saying things like, "I can see you bringing much good into your world. You have a heart to care for the needy. You have a sharp mind to help other people solve difficult problems."

In ancient cultures, the father pronounced a blessing over each of his children. This blessing was a pivotal event in a child's life. We continue this practice, not so much with a onetime event, but with the words we use every day. Those words, pregnant with purpose, will give birth to a ripple effect that will touch future generations.

Unfortunately, some of us missed out on this blessing from our own earthly father. And yet, God provides. Drink deeply from the affirmation that our heavenly Father gives us. With it comes the power to bless the children He has given us.

Father in heaven, show me what You think and feel about me. Empower me to use my words to bless my children. Let that blessing bring much good into their lives. Amen.

THE GIFT OF PEACE

"Peace I leave with you; my peace I give you."
JOHN 14:27 NIV

Even before they can talk, children are attuned to the emotional vibes of the family. They can sense that things are settled and happy or in a state of tension and chaos. Fathers lead the way in this regard. If a father is happy, the family tends to be happy. If he is at peace, he gives his children the priceless gift of peace. But a dad's tension and anger produce unrest.

We all have experienced times when we were not at peace. Stress in the workplace, tensions in marriage, health problems, financial trouble—all of these conspire to rob us of tranquility. In addition, unresolved issues from the past—like geologic fault lines in our souls—threaten our composure when something comes along to trigger us.

How do we find peace in an imperfect world? It starts when we make a practice of lifting every stressful experience up to God and asking Him for His perspective on it. As our heavenly Father, He conveys His peace to us, so that we can bring it home to our families. It's like this: a tiny canoe in the middle of the ocean is thrown around by every little wave, but a huge aircraft carrier slices through stormy seas with ease; the turbulence barely registers. In the same way, as we grow in Christ, our peace grows. The things that previously set us off no longer bother us. We're able to respond to crying babies, grouchy kids, surly teens, and burned toast with equanimity and good cheer. It's all part of the great adventure. We've found the secret. The power of God's perspective sets us free to be at peace.

Father in heaven, please show me how to get Your perspective on the things that stress me out. Give me the courage to look honestly at myself, and grant me the grace to receive from You the peace that is beyond all understanding. Amen.

THE TRUTH ABOUT FAILURE

*We who are strong have an obligation
to bear with the failings of the weak.*
ROMANS 15:1 ESV

During a major construction project, there was a mix-up and a manager ordered a crew to pour concrete before the necessary inspections had been made. By the time the manager discovered his mistake, the concrete was rock hard. Jackhammers would be needed to remove it. His mistake would cost his company more than a million dollars and jeopardize the production schedule for the entire project. With much fear, he went to the office of the CEO and reported what he had done. *I'm finished,* he told himself. Not only will I get fired, but no construction company will ever hire me again. The CEO listened to his entire report, along with his apology. After a long silence, he said, "People who never make mistakes never get anything done." The meeting was over. The manager kept his job and went on to have a long and successful career.

Making mistakes is part of the human experience.

Our children will fail. They won't win every football game. They may bring home an F on a report card. The police may show up at the door. A teenage daughter may break the news that she's pregnant.

Our children's mistakes—large or small—provide us with opportunities to fortify our children with the truth: "You got an *F* on a report card, not an *F* in life." "You made a bad decision. We've all made bad decisions. We learn from them, and we grow." "This setback does not define you. I am with you. We will tackle this thing together." In short, we treat our children as our Father in heaven treats us. We are not defined by our mistakes but rather by God's redemptive love.

God, thank You for loving me in spite of my failures. Thank You for using my mistakes as an opportunity to mold me into a better person. Empower me to encourage my children when they stumble. May they never be defined by their mistakes. Amen.

THE LANGUAGE OF LOVE

*Love (God's love in us) does not insist on its own rights
or its own way, for it is not self-seeking.*
1 CORINTHIANS 13:5 AMP

One father was trying to build a relationship with
his young son, who didn't want to be hugged, didn't
like to talk, and showed little interest in sports. Gifts
meant nothing to him. One day, soon after the family
moved to a new town, the dad took his son for a walk.
Few words were spoken as they walked to the edge
of town, sat down in a field, and watched the clouds
go by. After a while, they stood up and walked home.
Later, the boy said to his dad, "That was the best time
I ever had."

We all experience love in our own way. Words
of validation that one child drinks up may mean
nothing to another child. A daughter may treasure
forever a gift carefully selected for her, while a son in
the same family might ask himself, *Why is my dad
trying to buy my love? Why won't he just spend time
with me?* Some children thrive on wrestling and hugs,
kisses and pillow fights. Others tune in when we take

time to help with a school project. Some kids love to joke and laugh, while others feel disrespected by the same behavior. Some love to hug, and some want no one, including Dad, in their personal space. Some daughters love to go on a daddy date, while others would rather not. The language of love varies from person to person. As dads, we must learn to translate our love into the words and actions that will mean the most to each of our children.

God Himself recognizes our language of love and speaks it fluently. As we love our children as individuals, we pave the way for them to experience the love of God.

Heavenly Father, thank You for allowing me to experience Your love. Please teach me my children's language of love so that they may feel deeply loved both by me and by You. Amen.

CULTIVATOR OF DREAMS

His father wondered what the dreams meant.
GENESIS 37:11 NLT

"What do you see?" a man asked his young son.

"A stick," the son replied.

The man smiled as he pierced the soil with the stick and drove it into the ground in the backyard. "I see a willow tree," he said.

The next day, the boy ran outside. Nothing had changed. The stick was still just a stick. Soon the boy forgot all about the branch his father had planted; but, over time, the branch took root, and a new tree formed. By the time the boy was a young man, the willow tree towered over him, dominating the backyard.

Some people see sticks; God sees trees. He sees what could be, and He puts a vision for a better tomorrow into the hearts of His children. God puts a snapshot of the future into the minds of our children in the form of dreams, goals, and plans.

As dads, we have the privilege of cultivating those dreams. We understand that even a strong oak tree starts as a flimsy sapling, so we nurture our children's dreams when they are still delicate and fragile. We encourage our children, and imagine possibilities with them. We resist the temptation to force them to be something or someone they are not. We teach them to persevere, to dig deep and reach high, to build a proper foundation and achieve what no one else will ever accomplish.

When we cultivate a child's dreams, we set into motion a series of events that will change the course of many lives. As we release our children to achieve their dreams, we stand back and smile. God is at work. He is creating a better tomorrow for the people He loves.

Father in heaven, thank You for planting good dreams in the heart of my child. Give me the ability to cultivate those dreams so that my child will be empowered to do the good work You intend. Amen.

THERE ALL ALONG

*Every good and perfect gift is from above,
coming down from the Father of the heavenly lights,
who does not change like shifting shadows.*
JAMES 1:17 NIV

The experiences we have raising our children can teach us important spiritual principles. For example, one dad shared this story: "When my children were young, they loved candy, like most kids do. We knew that a little bit of candy was okay, but too much wasn't good for their health and for everybody's sanity. This presented a problem. Sometimes the kids had reached their sugar limit for the day about the same time my own sweet tooth kicked in. My wife and I didn't eat candy, but we wanted dessert. However, if we served ourselves a treat, our children would feel that they deserved one as well. We discovered a way around this problem. If we cut our ice cream into rectangular shapes and ate it from a plate with a knife and fork, our children never realized what we were doing. We were simply doing irrelevant adult things. Here we were, sitting at the same table, and they had no idea what they were missing. That didn't last forever, of course. One day they caught on. 'Hey, you guys have ice cream!' "

Sometimes the best things in life are right in front of us. They can remain hidden, not because they aren't there but because our eyes haven't been trained to see them. For example, most of us know that God loves us unconditionally. But one day God brings that into focus for us, and we begin to see His love everywhere—in the sunrise, in the eyes of our children, in the quiet voice of God's Spirit deep in our hearts. Once we see what God has placed right in front of us, our world will never again look the same.

Father in heaven, open my eyes. Empower me to see the good gifts You have placed right in front of me. I thank You for the beautiful gift of life. Amen.

Monsters in the Closet

"Never will I leave you; never will I forsake you."
HEBREWS 13:5 NIV

Most dads know this territory well: leaving a hall light on or checking the closet and under the bed to assure a frightened child that no monsters are lurking about. Most children go through a stage when they are afraid of things that simply aren't there. But we go through the motions because we understand that no amount of reasoning will dissuade a child whose world is inhabited by these imaginary things. Many times our children require reassurance rather than logic.

That's the case with adults sometimes as well. Our world is also inhabited by monsters—those hidden in the closets of our souls. No, they aren't big, green, hairy creatures with multiple legs and distorted faces. They take the form of guilt we can't seem to erase, feelings of incompetence, fears, and isolation. They stem from traumas and tangled-up events from the past, from put-downs that still echo in our minds. We may struggle to forgive ourselves. We may mask our pain with anger or addiction.

Logically speaking, we know that our monsters are just illusions, but that logic doesn't help us any more than it helps our children. We, too, need reassurance.

The transformation we need comes from inviting Jesus into the closets of our souls to confront the monsters we fear. Only He can give us the power to forgive ourselves, to know who we really are and what we're really capable of, to let go of fear and know that He is always there. As men, we are called upon to slay dragons—our own dragons. But we're not asked to do it alone. This is something that Jesus does with us. All it requires is the courage to open that closet door with Him.

Jesus, I open the door of my soul to You. Thank You for being here with me when I'm confronted with things I'm afraid to face alone. Show me what's real; protect me with Your reassuring truth. Amen.

MAKING REPAIRS

Jesus went everywhere doing good.
ACTS 10:38 ERV

Headlines scream bad news. Tragedy strikes close to home. No one can live long on this planet without coming face-to-face with reality: our world is broken. Things are not as they should be. But into this messed-up world, God arrives with tools in hand to make repairs. We see it in the life of Jesus. No matter what challenge was thrown at Him—hunger, disease, hatred, hurt, or sin—He found a way to fix it. He even repaired the damage done by death when He rose from the grave. When He ascended, He promised to return to set everything right. Meanwhile, God is still in the repair business. He still rebuilds the things that are damaged in our world.

How does He do this? He invites us to join Him. We are His agents, using the influence we have to fix things that are broken, to heal the hurting, while bringing justice, mercy, and good into our world. Every time we mend something that is in disrepair, we are an object lesson to our children. The world is not as it could be, but we join Jesus in making things right. Of course, fixing comes in many forms. Sometimes it means patching a bicycle tire. Sometimes it means holding a sobbing child. It may mean rebuilding an engine or restoring a relationship.

When we invest in the lives of our children by setting things right, we set up a pattern for them to follow throughout their lives. It may take time and effort and skill, but broken things can be fixed. When we take the time to make things right, we do more than give our children a virus-free computer or a toy train that chugs along a track. We give them hope.

Father in heaven, thank You for inviting me to join You as You make things right in this broken world. Please empower me to bring hope and encouragement to my children by fixing those things that need repair. Amen.

CHANGING DIAPERS

If we confess our sins to God, he can always be
trusted to forgive us and take our sins away.
1 JOHN 1:9 CEV

We all stumble from time to time. We make mistakes. We take the easy way out. We sin. This is something we all have in common. What matters most is what we do after we stumble. Some go into denial, refusing to face their own fallibility. Others use anger as a smoke screen, blaming everyone else for their own failings. Some hide behind an addiction. But it takes courage to look in the mirror and honestly face both the man and the mess.

"I was wrong. I'm sorry." Those are incredibly difficult words for many of us, but they are necessary words. They pave the way for our wrongs to be righted, for our sins to be forgiven, for our relationships to be restored. Facing God and our fellow human beings with a confession and an apology is a necessary step in our journey. Life cannot move forward unless and until we take that step of courage.

What makes confession so difficult? Why do

so many men avoid it at all costs? It would seem we secretly believe that a failure invalidates us as human beings. Perhaps we expect to be measured by our mistakes rather than honored for our honesty.

One way to look at this is to think about diapers. Most dads have changed many, many diapers. But when we look into the eyes of our children, we don't think about the diapers we've changed. We never even give that a second thought, because our children mean so much to us. In the same way, when we've sinned, God needs to deal with our sin and do what needs to be done so we can be clean again. But when He looks at us, He never thinks about our mistakes. Instead He sees the sons He loves.

God, give me the courage to be straight with You,
to be honest about my own failings.
Open my eyes to see how You really see me.
Forgive my sins and make me clean. Amen.

WHEN OUR CHILDREN STUMBLE

*At the right time we will harvest a good
crop if we don't give up, or quit.*
GALATIANS 6:9 MSG

Most of us—maybe all of us—expect to raise children
who are always obedient, never get into trouble,
never get caught in any of the many traps that lay
strewn across the landscape of a fallen world. But the
reality is that parenting takes place with real people—
parents who make mistakes and children who make
mistakes.

Real people face real problems. The police show
up at the door. The news is not good. Life takes an
unexpected detour, and our heads are spinning as we
try to keep up, because we never saw it coming.

It's in these moments that our faith can be our
greatest ally. God—and only God—can take the
threads of a disaster and weave them into something
beautiful. He constantly searches for ways to redeem
our failures and bring about something good. That's
why we never stop believing. That's why we never
lose hope. God is still working wonders.

But faith is not just a private affair. Throughout history, God has organized His followers into communities of faith. And for good reason: real men reach out for help. The wisdom and faith of others can help sustain us in our moments of greatest challenge, just as we will help others in their hour of need.

Our faith also teaches us that there is still much good, even in a child who has gone astray. We look for that good. We focus on it. We nurture it. We keep the relationship strong because we know that sowing good into a relationship means that we will reap good back if we don't give up. We persist because we see what others might not see: a better future.

God, grant me the faith to see beyond my present circumstances. Allow me to see Your good purposes alive in my life and in my children. Open my eyes to see their strengths, and give me the grace to keep my relationships with them strong. Amen.

HONORING IMPERFECT FATHERS

"Honor your father and your mother,
that your days may be long in the land
that the LORD your God is giving you."
EXODUS 20:12 ESV

In our culture, dads have a less than stellar track record. Too many are absent, abusive, or aloof. That means, for many, honoring the father in their lives is a challenge. And yet, the Bible commands it. We also know that doing so can set us free from the trap of bitterness, create a culture of respect that we can pass on to future generations, and open the door for us to receive more of the good gifts God has for us. So how do we find the grace to honor a father who made significant mistakes as a parent?

It starts with the realization that our fathers are given to us by God Himself. Sometimes that realization doesn't hit home until the end of a dad's life. As we ponder our relationships with our own fathers, flawed as they may be, a few things come into focus. Dads aren't perfect—many are far from it—but God has used their strengths and their mistakes to mold us into the men He wants us to be. And we, too, can honor our dads in light of how God has used their inadequate, possibly even hurtful, behaviors to help us become better fathers to our own children.

That doesn't mean we haven't been hurt or that there won't be a need to forgive our earthly fathers. We can't live in denial. We look squarely at the truth. But as we find the grace to release our resentment and give it to God, we create space to see the good that God has brought into our lives through our dads. And in that space, honor will grow.

Thank You, God, for the dad You gave me. Show me how to honor him in a way that pleases You. I pray that a culture of respect will be passed on to my children and to future generations. Amen.

THE JOURNEY TO FATHERHOOD

*He endured the shame of being nailed to a cross,
because he knew that later on he would be glad he did.*
HEBREWS 12:2 CEV

Most men don't grow up playing house, nor do we
start our adult lives imagining ourselves as dads.
Our minds might be on college, career, and marriage,
but the final step to family is a big one. Something
needs to change inside us before we are fully
prepared for the challenge. One dad describes the
change like this: "I remember the moment when I
first wanted to be a father. I was taking a walk on a
trail out in the country. It was a clear, crisp winter
day, and a fresh blanket of snow covered everything.
A couple hundred yards away, four young children
were sledding down a hill. I suddenly felt a strong
urge to join in on the fun, to celebrate life together
with them. I knew, of course, that I couldn't. So I just
watched them for a minute or two from a distance,
and then went on with my walk. At that point, I
realized something I had never known before. I
wanted to be a father."

Among men, the joy of being a dad is a closely guarded secret. Most men don't talk about it; most men don't know how to talk about it. But those of us who have made the magical transition from man to daddy are welcomed into an inner circle where we know that fatherhood is much, much more than the sum of soccer games and ballet lessons. Everything about our children gives life a deeper, richer shade of meaning.

That's no surprise, when we stop and think about it. Two thousand years ago, Jesus Christ weighed the options and made the tough choice; He chose to die. God gave what was most precious to Him, so that He could have what He wanted most: children.

God, thank You for the gift of life. Thank You for deciding that it was worth it to have children. Thank You for allowing me to be part of Your plan and giving me the privilege of caring for children You love. Amen.

STRANGE EXPECTATIONS

"I don't speak to you as my servants.
I speak to you as my friends."
JOHN 15:15 CEV

"If I ever have kids, I'm gonna make 'em behave,"
a young man said to his friends.

Sometimes we enter the world of fatherhood
with strange expectations. In the case of the young
man who made this statement, all his thoughts
about becoming the police officer of the family went
right out the window the first time he picked up
his newborn daughter. Almost instantly he realized
that being a daddy is much, much bigger than "Pick
up your toys"; "Take out the trash"; "Say please and
thank you"; and "Be home by curfew."

Is obedience important? Of course it is. But
being a daddy is about caring for the heart, soul,
and body of a fragile fellow human being. It's
about defending, protecting, encouraging, helping,
inspiring, coaching, nurturing, and providing.
"Behaving" is only a small sliver in the pie.

This distinction is important to understand,

because many people have reduced their relationship with God to bald obedience. Have I obeyed God today? Am I sinning, or am I righteous? Yes, it is important to steer clear of lust, gossip, and greed. But God is interested in far more than just managing our behavior. He is the caretaker of our dreams, the guardian of our future, the cheerleader of our present, and the healer of our past. He wants to move beyond a list of dos and don'ts to a rich and meaningful relationship with us.

For some, this is a paradigm shift. It means refocusing on relationship, taking time to listen, and sharing our thoughts and feelings with a Father who is so much more than a heavenly policeman. It means opening the door to our world and inviting God to move in.

Dear Father in heaven, I want to obey You.
But I want You to have more than just my obedience.
I want You to have all of me. I want You to feel
welcome and honored in my world, so our relationship
can be all that You want it to be. Amen.

HONOR IS A GIFT

Give to everyone what you owe them. . .
if honor, then honor.
ROMANS 13:7 NIV

We want our children to honor their parents, not because we're on some kind of ego trip but because we know this is what is best for them. As children respect their dads, it places them in a better position to benefit from the wisdom that our years of experience bring. Listening makes children teachable, and teachability spares young people a world of pain. We explain to our children that honor is a gift we give to other people. But it's a gift that rebounds to us. When people in authority are dishonored, they may scramble to protect their positions of responsibility, creating an adversarial "us versus them" relationship; but respect disarms this confrontational tone.

By esteeming their parents, children acknowledge that God puts imperfect people in positions of leadership and that someday they, too, will be placed in a similar position. As we teach our children to respect others, particularly their parents, we set them up to receive God's love and experience a deeper relationship with Him.

The Bible tells the story of a man who was misjudged by his brother, scorned by his wife, and hunted down like a criminal by his boss. His sons betrayed him, and for much of his life he was a fugitive and a wanted man. How did he respond to all of this? With honor. He showed respect to his boss, and when others wanted to harm that supervisor, he refused to allow it. When his boss came to a violent end, he mourned deeply. Again and again, he honored God and those who frequently didn't "deserve" honor. Where did all of this leave him? He became one of the greatest men who ever lived: King David.

God, help me to create a culture of respect in my home. Help each member of my family to give You the honor You deserve. Show me how to inspire my children to esteem their parents and honor one another. Amen.

WHEN "NO" MEANS LOVE

Love does not delight in evil but rejoices with the truth.
1 CORINTHIANS 13:6 NIV

Some years ago, a group of school administrators noticed that kids at school gathered at the fence separating the school property from the rest of the world. The administrators didn't feel it was healthy behavior, so they tried an experiment. They removed the fence. The effect was different than what they predicted. The kids seemed lost. They milled around in small groups close to the school building. The fence, social scientists concluded, provided security. Once the fence was gone, the feeling of security went with it.

As dads, we put up "fences" for our kids. We need to place boundaries on their behavior for their own safety and well-being. Being a dad sometimes requires us to take an unpopular stand with our children. We can't always say yes. We may need to say no to that extra piece of candy, or we may need to tell a teen that the party that "everybody" is going to is off-limits. Navigating through those tough conversations is never easy. Our children may not understand why we are refusing to grant them the permission they desire. But we have a responsibility for our children, and we sometimes need to draw the line and say, "No." It comes with the territory.

"No" is also part of God's vocabulary. It isn't the only word He uses. He loves to say yes. But when we experience a no from God, how can we perceive that refusal as an act of love? We start with honesty. We tell Him how the no feels and why it makes us feel the way it does. Then we listen and learn. Maybe the no is just a stepping-stone to a much bigger and better yes.

God, I want to share with You what I experience when You say no. Thank You that no is part of Your vocabulary of love. Empower me to understand Your heart toward me. Amen.

Preparing for Any Emergency

All who obey you should pray to you while they
still can. When troubles rise like a flood,
they will not reach them.
Psalm 32:6 ncv

Preparation is everything. We don't wait until the
house is engulfed in flames before we go out and buy
a fire extinguisher. We don't wait for the tornado to
strike before we determine the safest place of shelter.

People who train military personnel and police
officers understand that people in a crisis situation
will respond as they've been conditioned to respond.
The truth of this was made clear years ago when a
police officer was shot in the middle of a gunfight
because he was frantically looking around for a can
in which to place his empty shell casings. After that,
law enforcement training agencies reevaluated their
approach and made their training more realistic.
Likewise, martial artists practice the same technique
over and over again so that if they ever need to use
it in real life, their response is automatic. It's called
muscle memory. They don't need to think about it;

they just do it.

How do we prepare spiritually for those moments when our world is turned upside down? We understand that God is our first and last line of defense in any kind of crisis. We need the spiritual "muscle memory" of turning to God in times of need. This is one reason why we put certain spiritual rhythms in our lives. We make a practice of nourishing our souls with God's words from the Bible. We make a habit of taking our needs and the needs of our families to God in prayer. We know that an enduring relationship with God is far more than a "foxhole faith." When we are secure in our relationship with God, we never go through a crisis alone.

God, I don't know what the future might bring,
but I do know that I don't want to face it without You.
Please keep me close to You, and carry my family
through any crisis we may experience. Amen.

GETTING OUR CHANCE

*Let us not become weary in doing good,
for at the proper time we will reap
a harvest if we do not give up.*
GALATIANS 6:9 NIV

As dads, we know that everyone deserves a chance to take a shot and make a difference. At age two, Jason McElwain was diagnosed as autistic. As a high school student, he desperately wanted to be a basketball player. But between his five-foot six-inch stature and his autism, the only role he could find on the team was that of manager. At age seventeen, he ran the clock, kept statistics, and carried water bottles to the players. But he did this with such enthusiasm that the coach decided to reward him with some time on the court. He just needed to find the right moment.

That moment came when the team was playing an old rival. With four and a half minutes left in the game, Jason's team was up by twenty points. It seemed safe to let him play, so the coach pointed to him and said the words that Jason had waited his entire high school career to hear: "You're in."

He got the ball early, took a shot and missed. He tried again and failed. You could feel the tension in the crowd. On the sidelines, people were silently praying, *Please, God, let him make a shot.* Then, with three minutes and twelve seconds left on the clock, something magical happened. The ball traveled from Jason's hands, arced through the air, and—swish!—dropped through the basket. Everyone was on their feet cheering. But it didn't stop there. Now that he was dialed in, Jason made shot after shot. When the final buzzer sounded, he had scored twenty points for his team.

The God we serve deeply understands our need for a few minutes on the court. He hasn't forgotten. We will each get a chance to make a difference.

Thank You, God, that You give everyone a chance to play in the game of life. Thank You for those moments You give my children—and me—on the court. Empower me to use my time for Your glory. Amen.

Unexpected Help

Where will I find help? It will come from the Lord,
who created the heavens and the earth.
Psalm 121:1–2 CEV

Life is full of surprises. For Sara Tucholsky, the
unexpected happened three times in one day. Sara
played softball for Western Oregon University. At
five feet two inches tall, she was anything but a
heavy hitter. Line drives were her specialty. She had
never hit a home run in her life. But one day in 2008,
while playing against Central Washington, a miracle
happened, and the ball sailed over the fence. With
both teams fighting for the conference championship,
these three RBIs mattered. As Sara started to run
around the bases, in her excitement she forgot to
tag first base. Realizing her mistake, she whirled
around—and that's when the unthinkable happened.
Her knee blew out, and she dropped to the ground
in excruciating pain. Slowly, she crawled back to first
base, where she remained, unable to move.

What to do? The umpires ruled that if she
didn't complete the run around the bases, her home

run would be reduced to a two-run single. If her teammates helped her, she would be called out.

That's when Mallory Holtman, Central Washington's first baseman and career home run leader, stepped forward with an idea. After a hasty conference with the umpire, Mallory's plan was approved. Moments later, she and one of her teammates, Liz Wallace, gently lifted Sara and carried her around the bases, pausing at each one to allow Sara to tag it with her uninjured foot. Only about a hundred people were at the game to witness this stunning act of kindness, but word quickly spread, and for the next several weeks it made headlines all over the nation.

This act of kindness reminds us of the kind of God we serve. When parenting and life bring us to the end of our resources, God—in ways we would never expect—carries us home.

Father, thank You for seeing and knowing the limits of what we can do. Thank You that when we fall, You don't leave us stranded. Thank You that You carry us home. Amen.

CROSSING THE FINISH LINE

*My only aim is to finish the race and complete
the task the Lord Jesus has given me.*
ACTS 20:24 NIV

Runner Derek Redmond was one of Britain's stars in
the 400-meter dash. Twice he had set a new British
record in the event. Despite numerous injuries and
eight surgeries, he had come back to win a world
championship and was now poised to win big at the
1992 Summer Olympic Games in Barcelona, Spain.

Two hundred and twenty-five meters into the
semifinals, Redmond's hopes for a gold medal were
dashed when a new injury to his left hamstring
forced him to his knees. Alone on the track with
65,000 people in the stands and millions watching
by television, Redmond struggled to his feet with one
goal in mind: to get to the finish line.

So much of life is about finishing. As fathers,
one of the biggest gifts we can give our children is to
finish well and teach them to do the same.

Apparently, Derek's father, Jim Redmond, had
the same idea. Waving aside the security guards

around the track, Jim jumped over the rail and ran toward Derek. "That's my son," he yelled, "and I'm going to help him."

Derek Redmond didn't win a medal that day, but that moment has been celebrated as one of the most-remembered moments in Olympic history.

Like Derek Redmond, we started out well. But then we stumbled. The race we wanted to win, we lost. Our Father in heaven could have stayed in the stands and let us fight it out on our own. But He didn't. Instead, God clothed Himself with human flesh, jumped the rail, and joined us on the track. Together we will cross the finish line.

Jesus, thank You for not staying in the stands. Thank You for not leaving me injured and alone on the track. I invite You into my life. Let's finish this race together. Amen.

NEVER GIVE UP

Love never gives up, never loses faith, is always hopeful, and endures through every circumstance.
1 CORINTHIANS 13:7 NLT

"I was a great parent until I had kids." The man who said this reflects what we all know to be true: there are no perfect dads. Parenting happens in real time with real people. In the mix of the moment, mistakes are made.

Let's face it: sometimes we're clueless. Children don't come with an owner's manual, and every child presents unique challenges. We're figuring it out on the fly. The ship of parenting is built mostly at sea.

This is where a mixture of humility and hardheaded stubbornness serves us well. We need enough humility to recognize when we've made a mistake, to apologize, to make things right. But we also need enough tough-minded determination to get back in the game, even when we get knocked down. Parenting isn't easy. But we don't bail. We stay in for the long haul, even when we feel like throwing in the towel.

Winston Churchill became one of the towering figures of the twentieth century because he recognized the threat of Nazi aggression long before it was the popular view. Later, when England stood alone against the most powerful military coalition of that day, Churchill dug in his heels and declared, "Never give in—never, never, never, never, in nothing great or small, large or petty, never give in.... Never yield to force; never yield to the apparently overwhelming might of the enemy."

We persevere because that's what Jesus did for us. He didn't feel like going to the cross, but He did it anyway. He showed us the way when He put aside His comfort and safety and stepped out in front of the train of humanity's hatred to take the hit for us.

God, empower me to persevere.
I want to be the best dad I can be,
but I know I'm human. I know I'll make mistakes.
That's why I need You to pick me up when I fall
and give me the determination to get back
in the game to win. Amen.

WHEN GOD SPEAKS

You have taught children and infants to tell
of your strength, silencing your enemies
and all who oppose you.
PSALM 8:2 NLT

One day, in northern India, a group of militants
gathered around a Christian school, shouting
accusations and threats. The leader of the school
stepped outside to calm the crowd, but his efforts
backfired when the mob dragged him into their
midst and started beating him. He was the father of
a baby girl. This child was old enough to walk but
could only speak a word or two. In the confusion
that followed, she somehow slipped away from her
caretaker and wandered out to the crowd to see what
was happening to her father.

Just in time, one of the women from the school
saw her. This little girl was in terrible danger. So the
woman ran outside, swooped up the baby, and dashed
to the women's dormitory. She got inside and locked
the door just ahead of the furious mob.

Enraged, the persecutors tried to break down

the door. When that didn't work, they doused the building with kerosene and tried to set it on fire, while the women inside screamed in understandable hysteria.

In the midst of this chaos, the frightened women heard a tiny voice. It was the little girl. She said, " 'Why are you so afraid? Don't you know that you are the apple of My eye?' " In that moment, the scene inside was transformed. Terror gave way to peace. Screaming changed to songs of praise. After several unsuccessful attempts to burn the building down, the crowd dispersed.

How do we hear the voice of God? We hear it in unexpected places at unexpected times. If we're listening carefully, sooner or later we hear it in the words of our children. When that happens, time stands still, and we know we are in the presence of God.

Dear God, open my ears to hear Your voice.
Let me recognize what You are teaching me
through the children You have given me.
Thank You for being present in my family.
Amen.

REFUELING SELF-ESTEEM

He gave them the right to be the children of God.
JOHN 1:12 CEV

With high-powered impact wrenches driven by compressed nitrogen, a NASCAR pit crew can change all four tires in less than twenty seconds. Their whole mission is to get their driver back on the track as quickly and safely as possible.

Sometimes being a dad is like being on a NASCAR pit crew. Our job is to get our children back into the race. With statements like, "You are capable"; "You are beautiful"; "You can do it"; "I believe in you," we refuel their self-esteem and strengthen our kids for the road ahead.

Some people worry that complimenting children will swell their pride, transfer their confidence from God to self, and rob them of needed humility. In practice, however, the opposite is true. Insecurity often drives pride and false humility. Children with healthy self-esteem know their place in the world. They aren't easily discouraged or deterred from achieving their God-given purpose. Children with strong self-esteem know they're loved, capable, and lovely. This makes them much less susceptible to negative peer pressure, life-controlling issues, exploitation, and manipulation. It's a tough world out there, but we can equip our kids to be tough enough to thrive in it if we teach them who they really are.

Children, even the ones who seem to be ignoring us, are constantly looking to their dads for affirmation. One father started signing all his letters and e-mails to his adult daughter with "I'm proud of you." That simple change has transformed their relationship.

When we build our children's self-esteem, we emulate what God has done for us. The Bible is clear. We are created to live forever, designed to make a difference. We carry God's presence into the world. We are the triumphant sons of God.

God, empower me to tell my children the truth about who they really are so they may carry Your presence into the world with confidence and determination. Thank You. Amen.

Overcoming Hardships

Put up with hard times. God uses them to train you.
HEBREWS 12:7 NIrV

On the morning of June 6, 1944, 156,000 Allied troops fought their way onto the beaches of Normandy, France. The scene was a mixture of horror and chaos as the carefully laid plans of Operation Overlord met with bad weather, human error, and the relentless resistance of a determined military foe. Even though there were no safe places, each soldier, sailor, airman, and marine pressed on, drawing on every ounce of courage they could muster. After enormous sacrifice and countless acts of bravery, these troops secured a foothold on the Continent, pushed back the occupying army of Nazi Germany, and liberated Europe from Hitler's domination.

While we admire the heroism of our forefathers, we are also sobered because we never know what kinds of challenges a new generation will face. How do we prepare our children for an uncertain future?

Part of that preparation involves giving our children a chance to work their way through tough situations. Age-appropriate challenges present our children with opportunities to learn and grow strong. The story is told of a young boy who observed a butterfly just beginning to emerge from its cocoon. Seeing how the creature was struggling to get free, the boy thought to help the butterfly by cutting the cocoon open. The result? The butterfly emerged with a swollen body and shriveled wings. Robbed of the opportunity to struggle, the butterfly was unable to force the fluid from its body into its wings. It remained like that—crawling around, unable to fly—until it finally died.

In our own faith journeys, we often take our biggest steps forward as a result of trials. They strengthen us for whatever the future may hold. The opportunity to struggle and overcome—that is a gift from God.

Thank You, God, for the opportunity to struggle and overcome. Thank You for teaching us the value of depending on You when times are bad as well as good. Amen.

FINDING TIME

There is a time for everything.
ECCLESIASTES 3:1 NIV

How do kids spell love? T-I-M-E. Many children measure how much they are valued and cared for by the minutes and hours that moms and dads give them undivided attention. One successful father said, "I used to get upset when my neighbor kids made such a big deal over their dad coming home from work. Why didn't my kids celebrate my arrival? One day I realized the answer. My neighbor's kids were starved for their dad's attention. My own children got a healthy dose of it every day."

How do we do it? The responsibilities of everyday life can easily fill twenty-four hours a day before we even factor in one or more children. How do we create time for our kids?

It helps to embrace interruptions. Kids live in the now. They have no idea that we're on a schedule. They just know that, in this moment, either we care enough to listen or we don't. When we study the life of Jesus, we discover that most of His greatest moments were interruptions—Zacchaeus, Bartimaeus, Jairus, the calming of the sea—all of these and many more recorded events were departures from His itinerary. But He didn't seem to mind. In fact, it seemed that Jesus thrived on interruptions, having the ability to see the potential of each new opportunity.

It may not be convenient, but our children need our undivided attention. That means setting aside the phone, turning off the TV, putting down the newspaper, and actively listening. We may not always be able to give our children the time they desire, but each moment we share with them is both a gift and an investment. It reminds them and us that we have a Father in heaven who always has time for us.

God, grant me the ability to understand what's important in the now. Help me to shift my focus to my children when they need my attention. Enable me to give them the gift of time. Amen.

NEVER STOP GROWING

The hearts of the wise make their mouths prudent, and their lips promote instruction. Gracious words are a honeycomb, sweet to the soul and healing to the bones.
PROVERBS 16:23-24 NIV

The fruit doesn't fall far from the tree. Our children become what we are. We lead—positively or negatively—by our example far more than we do by our words or instructions. Modeling attitudes and behaviors for the next generation is one of the greatest gifts we can give. So, how do we become someone we would want our children to emulate?

One of the best ways to guide our children is by exemplifying teachability. Openness to instruction is important because it sets the stage for growth throughout life. The person who has stopped learning has stopped growing. In the classic Aesop fable "The Tortoise and the Hare," the tortoise wins the race because he keeps on going when the hare stops to nap. In similar fashion, the teachable person keeps on growing, even when others stop. When we are teachable, we hold the belief that every person and every circumstance has the power to teach us something, if we're willing to learn. A teachable man shows an active eagerness to improve, a lifelong quest to discover, and an ability to accept and evaluate criticism without getting defensive.

Teachability should not be confused with passivity or an inability to lead. We still pilot the ship even when we're looking for ways to improve. In the Bible, King David's sons were his royal advisers. He listened to their input so he could do his job of leading even better.

Sometimes it's difficult to learn, particularly from someone who doesn't treat us with respect. But if we're willing to listen, God is always willing to give us His perspective on other people and trying circumstances. Life's greatest lessons can come from the most unexpected places.

God, please open my mind and my heart to learn from other people and to recognize the lessons You have planted all around me. Let me pass the quality of teachability on to my children. Amen.

BUILDING OUR HOME

*"I'm going ahead of you to prepare
your eternal home."*
JOHN 14:2 TEB

A construction contractor called a crew leader into his office. "I'm putting you in charge of building a home," he said. "As with all our jobs, quality matters. This is important to me, and I'm trusting you to do the job right. Use the best materials, and use the best practices."

Unfortunately, the crew leader was less than trustworthy. He built the home, but he cut corners everywhere. Instead of insisting on excellence, he settled for mediocrity. After a few months, the job was done, and he reported back to his boss.

"Are you satisfied that you did your very best?" the owner of the company asked.

"Yes, sir," the crew leader replied.

"Good," the boss smiled as he handed him the keys, "because this is now your home. I had it built for you."

As dads, we are constantly building our own

homes. We're not necessarily building with two-by-fours, drywall, and siding, but rather with words, leadership, and acts of kindness. We understand this. We care. We want our homes to be as close to heaven as possible for our children.

It seems fitting that Jesus spent His young adult years as a carpenter. He knows how to build things that last. He has gone ahead of us to build a home for us in heaven. And that home is not mainly about streets of gold or mansions in glory. It's about building a place where we each will feel at home, where everyone will care and be cared about, where every person will experience the presence and love of God.

Jesus invites us to join His construction crew. We have a hand in building that eternal home by how we value and care for those God puts in our path, starting with our children.

Jesus, thank You for building an eternal home for us. Please empower me to build a strong home for my children where they will feel loved and cared for. Amen.

MIRACLE WAITING TO HAPPEN

I can do all things through him who strengthens me.
PHILIPPIANS 4:13 ESV

Every child is a miracle waiting to happen. Consider Michael. He was one of twelve children born to an alcoholic mother, who was also a crack-cocaine addict. His father, in and out of prison, was murdered when Michael was a teen. His parents left him to raise himself. He flunked first grade and then flunked second grade. He bounced from foster home to foster home, finally ending up on the streets as a homeless teen.

Hopeless, right? That's what most people thought, but one family disagreed. They invited Michael into their home. They saw his potential and cultivated it. They made sure he got the coaching he needed. They got him through high school and even managed to get him a scholarship to college. While at college, this young man, once considered hopeless, twice made the honor roll. But he's better known for his other achievements. He became a star football player, winning a string of college awards, after which he was drafted into the NFL. On February 3, 2013, Michael Oher helped his team, the Baltimore Ravens, win a Super Bowl championship. His life story became the subject of the 2009 feature film *The Blind Side*.

What transformed a throwaway teen into a national sports celebrity? Faith. Someone believed in him. Being a dad is about believing in our kids. It's about seeing their potential and opening their eyes to see it, too. It's opening the door for a new generation to achieve their dreams. God can do anything. He could do everything. But He doesn't. He hands the baton to us. The amazing thing here is not so much that we believe in God, but that He believes in us and sends us out to transform our world.

God, please open my eyes to see the potential
in my children. Show me how to encourage them,
and how to draw out the best in them.
Make me a good dad to my kids. Amen.

WRONG DIRECTION!

"Come to me, all of you who are tired and have heavy loads, and I will give you rest."
MATTHEW 11:28 NCV

On the evening of Tuesday, September 6, 2011, a train departed from Tirupati, India, with more than one thousand passengers aboard. The next morning, the train arrived 850 miles from its destination after traveling 608 miles in the wrong direction. An investigation revealed that a railroad employee had entered the wrong code, placing the train on the wrong track. Other railroad employees were literally sleeping on the job, so no one noticed the mistake until the next morning. Passengers and officials were both grateful and relieved that the train didn't collide with another train during the thirteen-hour journey away from their intended destination.

As dads, one of our biggest jobs is teaching our children to take the right track and travel in the right direction. Although numerous safeguards exist to keep trains, planes, and automobiles from going the wrong way, we humans are afflicted with damage to our internal navigation system. For us, it can be counterintuitive to travel in the right direction.

For example, when we stumble (as we all do), our natural tendency is to hide from God—just as Adam and Eve hid from God in the garden after eating the forbidden fruit. We hope to clean ourselves up so that God won't be disappointed with us. But that never works. We don't have the ability to clean up or dress up for God. Only God can make us clean.

This is why it's so important that we be thoughtful about how to respond to our children's mistakes and misbehavior. If our children see that our focus is on restoring them, then they can approach God with confidence. Instead of avoiding God, they can go to Him for restoration—and so can we.

Father in heaven, please help me to come to You when I least feel like it—and especially when I want to avoid You. Empower me to teach my children to do the same. Amen.

TEACHING INTEGRITY

*The power of the wicked will be broken,
but the LORD upholds the righteous.*
PSALM 37:17 NIV

Two maple trees stood in the family's backyard. They were about the same height, about the same age. In fact, on the outside, they looked alike in almost every respect. But there was a difference. One night, a violent storm swept across the state. The winds were high, a tornado warning was issued, and the family huddled in the basement. When the storm passed, their home was fine, but the backyard was not. One of their two maple trees had fallen, split right down the middle. In the light of the next day, it became clear why one tree stood up to the storm and the other did not. The heart of the fallen maple was rotted, which compromised the strength of the tree. The damaged tree was unhealthy on the inside.

On the outside, people, too, can look much alike. We don't get to see what's in their hearts. Sometimes it takes the storms of life to bring to the surface what is really there.

We build character in our kids, knowing that integrity is the best form of self-defense. We can overcome seemingly insurmountable obstacles if we are clear that our cause is just. What is integrity? It's the ability to keep a promise, even when it hurts. It's doing what's right when no one but God is watching. It's not taking the easy way out. Integrity empowers us to stand alone, when everyone else wants to do wrong. It's standing for the truth, whether it's in style or not. It's a refusal to be bought and a determination never to compromise with evil.

If our children grow up with a strong moral compass, they can filter through many options and choose the high road. It becomes a way of life for them.

God, please enable me to model and teach integrity to my children. Where I have fallen, empower me to make things right, and give us all grace to learn from our mistakes. Amen.

SOURCE OF CONFIDENCE

You try to get praise from each other,
but you do not try to get the praise that
comes from the only God. So how can you believe?
JOHN 5:44 NCV

Some people feel as if they need to have a certain title on their business card, a certain car in their driveway, a certain number on their paycheck, in order to feel okay about themselves. Others receive validation from trophies celebrating past accomplishments or the praise of friends and coworkers. Some look for affirmation in more destructive ways, through extramarital affairs or life-controlling addictions. Some tally up their good deeds or their religious activities.

Most people know that these external "measuring sticks" provide a fragile foundation for confidence and self-esteem. Money and prestige can be gone in an instant. Our past—good or bad—doesn't define us. We can never be good enough. Self-destructive choices haunt us instead of helping us.

Construction contractors build high by digging

deep. The higher the building, the more important the foundation. Likewise, confidence—that magical something that carries us through life's ups and downs—must rest on something solid. Our faith in God's ability to use us for good, and our own sense of being okay, depend on this foundation.

As dads, we want our children's confidence grounded in something strong enough to stand up to life's storms. But how do we establish a stable foundation? The path to confidence, ironically, travels straight through our insecurities. Every time we feel unsettled or off balance and we bring our secret fears to God, it's an opportunity for Him to tell us the truth about who we are, who He is, and how He feels about us. His perspective empowers us to live life on His terms, with overwhelming confidence in His power to carry us through.

God, when my children are insecure and afraid, empower us as a family to get Your perspective so that my kids can go through life filled with confidence based on Your truth. Amen.

REJOICING WITH OTHERS

When others are happy, be happy with them.
ROMANS 12:15 CEV

One of the greatest gifts we can give our children is freedom from jealousy. Envy destroys relationships, breaks up families, and can be the driving force behind all kinds of evil. In the Bible, resentment caused the young men in one family to sell their brother into slavery.

What drives this ill will? It comes from a mind-set of scarcity. In the Soviet gulag, prisoners sometimes murdered one another over a scrap of bread that most of us would refuse to eat. In the same way, brothers and sisters sometimes squabble, competing for what they think is a limited supply of parental love and approval.

Let's look at this from the other side. Imagine the world's wealthiest man. Would it upset him that his neighbor got a new car or that his best friend received a promotion at work? Not likely!

When things aren't going our way and others around us are receiving praise, gifts, and rewards, how do we find it in our hearts to rejoice with them over their success? We need God to show us all over again how wealthy we are in Him. As sons of God, we are members of the wealthiest family in the universe. There is no limit to what our Father in heaven will give us in His wisdom and in His timing.

This is why we shower our own children with love. We want them to know how much they are valued and cared for. We want them to be filled to overflowing with love and acceptance, partly so they can honestly smile and be glad when good things happen to others in their world. We want to be a conduit through which they can experience God's limitless love.

God, let me be a channel through which You can pour out Your love on my children. Let them experience the abundance of Your love so they will never be caught in the trap of small-minded scarcity. Amen.

STANDING TOGETHER

*"I pray also for those who will believe in me through
their message, that all of them may be one,
Father, just as you are in me and I am in you."*
JOHN 17:20–21 NIV

Two boys were fighting. Their father separated them,
took them out to the backyard, and told them to
gather up sticks that had fallen from a recent storm.
Taking some twine from the garage, the dad tied
the sticks together in a bundle and handed it to his
younger son. "Break this," he said. The boy strained to
break the bundle but failed. His older brother looked
on, confident that he could do better. But when his
turn came, he, too, found it impossible to break the
sticks when they were tied together. Pulling out a
jackknife, the father cut the string and handed each
boy individual sticks from the bundle. "Break these,"
he said. Apart from the bundle, the sticks broke with
ease. "These sticks are like members of a family," the
dad explained. "When we stand together, we stand
strong. But when we fight, when we are divided, we
lose the strength of family. We become easy targets."

Most of us know this old story—adapted from an Aesop fable. But most of us have little training or experience in building family unity. It's a tall order, particularly when the people living under one roof can be so completely at odds with one another at times.

As men, we lead the way in making family our priority. Many other things compete for our time, but it's hard to imagine anything more important than the people God has entrusted to our care. We model reconciliation, peacemaking, and conflict resolution for our children. We accentuate the strengths of each family member and openly express our appreciation for each person. We do these things because that's what Jesus has done for us. Apart from Him, we would squabble over our many differences. But He died to make us one.

God, please bring my family together.
Empower me to inspire loyalty and unity.
Forgive me when I am part of the conflict instead
of part of the solution. Make us one. Amen.

THE TEAM

*Each of us finds our meaning and
function as a part of his body.*
ROMANS 12:5 MSG

Rick Hoyt was born with cerebral palsy. During labor
and delivery, the umbilical cord was wrapped around
his neck, blocking the flow of oxygen to his brain. It
soon became clear that he would be a quadriplegic.
Doctors encouraged his parents to place him in
an institution, but his parents refused. They were
determined to give their son a full and rich life. At
age eleven, Rick was given a computer device that
enabled him to communicate, allowing him to attend
school. He not only went on to graduate from high
school but also from college, with a degree in special
education.

Meanwhile, something powerful was unfolding
in the life of his family. When Rick was fifteen years
old, his father, Dick, decided to enter a five-mile
race to benefit an athlete who had been paralyzed
in an accident. Even though Dick wasn't a runner,
he decided to run—not alone, but with his son. He

pushed Rick in a wheelchair. After their first race together, Rick said, "Dad, when I'm running, it feels like I'm not handicapped." Inspired to continue, Dick Hoyt trained incessantly, and the two entered more races. To date, they've competed in more than one thousand endurance events, including seventy marathons and several Ironman competitions. They even ran and biked across the United States. Team Hoyt, as they are called, was inducted into the Ironman Hall of Fame in 2008 and was honored with a bronze statue erected near the starting line of the Boston Marathon.

Without Rick, his dad would be just another runner. And without his dad, Rick would be just a guy with cerebral palsy. But together they have inspired, encouraged, and educated millions of people around the world. They perfectly illustrate what every dad instinctively knows: we need each other.

Thank You, God, for giving me a family. Thank You that we are far more together than we ever will be separately. Empower me to convey this important truth to my children by what I say and do. Amen.

God's Representative

*We are therefore Christ's ambassadors, as though
God were making his appeal through us.*
2 CORINTHIANS 5:20 NIV

Mahatma Gandhi once said, "If Christians would
really live according to the teachings of Christ, as
found in the Bible, all of India would be Christian
today." No doubt he was thinking of an infamous
experience he'd had as a young man in South
Africa. After studying law in England, Gandhi
worked as an attorney in South Africa. There he
became fascinated with the teachings of Jesus and
considered becoming a Christian. But his desire
to become a Christian came to an abrupt end one
day when he decided to visit a local church. A man
standing at the door barred him from entering. When
he patiently explained that he wanted to worship with
that congregation, he was called a derogatory name
(based on his race) and threatened with physical
expulsion if he didn't leave voluntarily.

We can argue that this tragic incident is yet
another example of imperfect people misrepresenting

a perfect God. From the Spanish Inquisition to the white supremacist movement, much has been said and done in the name of Jesus that has no connection to Him at all. There is wisdom in teaching our children that just because people might claim to represent Jesus doesn't mean they actually do.

But there is a more important reminder here for us as dads. We, as parents, are our children's first exposure to God. Everything we say and do models God to our impressionable young children, whether we want it to or not. How our children relate to us will form the foundation of how they relate to God. That's why our job is so important. Unlike the man who barred Gandhi's way into the church, we welcome our children to Jesus. We teach them who He is not just by our words but also by everything we do.

God, please work with me so that I can help my children know who You really are. Please empower me to lead my children to Jesus by what I say and what I do. Amen.

THE GIFT OF LAUGHTER

*[God] will yet fill your mouth with laughter
and your lips with shouts of joy.*
JOB 8:21 NIV

A large and important part of being a dad is having fun with our kids. Shared laughter is a precious gift we give our children. It builds emotional equity in our families, giving us the relational capital we need when it comes time to lead. Laughter soothes pain, defends against hurt, and brings families together.

Opportunities for fun are everywhere. Running through the lawn sprinkler on a hot summer day, pillow fights, long walks in the woods—creating laughter-filled memories doesn't need to cost anything but time. One dad hid loose change around the house and invited his children to keep whatever they found. Another dad divided up the Lincoln Logs and toy soldiers between his two sons. When Mom was away, they built forts for their soldiers and then attacked the enemy fortifications with a bag of marbles. Exploring a riverbank, building a tree house, organizing a neighborhood game of football—

the possibilities are endless. Sometimes these fun moments can happen spontaneously, like making silly faces in front of a mirror, or taking turns creating lines of audio for a muted television commercial.

There are boundaries, of course. We never laugh at someone else's expense. Humor at home is never meant to harm; and if it does, we heal the hurt right away. At the same time, as dads, we don't take ourselves too seriously. We let our children laugh with us. We know that there's a time to be goofy and there's a time to be serious.

Many people view God as deadly serious all the time. But inside the family of God, there is ample room for fun. Heaven will be, among other things, a place of laughter. God invented fun, and He knows how to laugh with us.

God, thank You for the gift of fun. Help me to create many happy, fun-filled memories with my children. Help us as a family to laugh together. I pray that my children will know You as the God who brings laughter. Amen.

LEARNING TO FORGIVE

Forgive, just as the Lord forgave you.
COLOSSIANS 3:13 NIV

Jim and John were going into business together. They each needed $5,000 to get the business started, but neither had any money. So they decided to borrow from family. Jim's family was struggling, but they managed to scrape up the money for him to borrow, contingent on his maintaining a strict repayment schedule. John's family had money to spare, and they easily wrote him a check for the full amount.

Unfortunately, the business failed, leaving Jim and John with nothing. They had to go back to their families and break the bad news. "I'm broke. I don't have the ability to repay this loan. I'm sorry. Is there any way you can cancel the debt?"

John's family said, "You tried your best. It didn't work out. Don't worry about it. We don't even miss the money." But Jim's family was in a different place. "We needed that money to pay our bills. Now that you can't repay us, how will we pay the rent or put food on the table?"

As Christians, we are called upon to "cancel the debt"; that is, to forgive those who hurt us. This is one of the most difficult requirements of the Christian life—and one of the most difficult lessons to teach our children. Why is it that some people are able to forgive with ease, while others struggle to forgive?

The answer has to do with our own spiritual wealth. If we've had a deep encounter with Christ in those places where we've been hurt, if we've been enriched with the certainty of who we really are in God's family, then forgiving others becomes manageable. We measure the hurt of their offense against the magnitude of God's love for us, and smile.

God, please enable me to be a channel of Your love to my children, so they will have the inner strength to withstand the storms of life. When they get hurt, bring Your comfort and reassurance to them. Empower them to forgive. Amen.

BREAKING BARRIERS

"The kingdom of heaven has been advancing with force. And forceful people are taking hold of it."
MATTHEW 11:12 NIrV

At 215 Montague Street in Brooklyn, New York, a plaque reads, "On August 28, 1945, Jackie Robinson, a rising star of the Negro Leagues, met with Branch Rickey, Dodger president and general manager, and signed an agreement to play in the Dodger organization. This initiated the process of becoming the first African-American player on a major-league baseball team—integrating the major leagues and making baseball truly the pastime of the entire nation."

Even once the agreement had been signed, it didn't come to fruition until April 15, 1947, when Robinson broke the "color barrier" that had prevented African Americans from playing in the major leagues and stepped out to play ball for the Brooklyn Dodgers. From that point forward, he endured taunting, racial slurs, hate mail, and worse. But he never lost his focus. He simply played great baseball.

His dedication paid off. By 1949, the Negro Leagues were virtually a thing of the past, as all the best players had been recruited into the major leagues. Robinson had proven to his generation what we take for granted today: African Americans could excel at anything, and baseball was no exception. It takes a certain kind of courage and foresight to break barriers and pioneer new territory. One or more of your children might be a Jackie Robinson of tomorrow, proving to their generation that the "impossible" can be done if one simply has the faith and dedication to do it.

This is why we take seriously the dreams of our children. This is why we give them opportunities to persevere through hardship to meet age-appropriate challenges. We are training them to create a better future, just as God is training us to pioneer new territory for Him.

God, please empower me to prepare my children for the challenges they will face. Give me the faith to believe that You can do the impossible through my children, and let me communicate that confidence to them. Amen.

RUNNING AWAY

*"You will know the truth, and
the truth will set you free."*
JOHN 8:32 ESV

A woman who had been shopping stepped out of
the store and got into her car. As she left the parking
lot, she noticed that a large truck was following her
closely. She turned left on the next street. The truck
turned as well. She sped up. The truck kept up. When
she slowed down to allow him to pass, he slowed
down and showed no interest in going around her.
By now she was becoming concerned. She pulled
onto the highway, and the truck followed. When
she changed lanes, he changed lanes also. Finally,
she took an exit and looked for a convenience store.
Pulling into the parking lot, she slammed on the
brakes, threw open her car door, and raced into the
store to summon help.

The truck driver also stopped, jumped out of
his truck, and ran toward the woman's vehicle. But
instead of following the woman into the store, he
wrestled to the ground the convicted rapist who had

been hiding on the floor of her backseat. From his vantage point high up in the cab of his truck, he had been able to see what the woman couldn't. He knew where the real danger lay.

For most people, the things we run from are our own fears, shame, and insecurity. As men, we tend to cover over these feelings with anger or push them away with denial. But we'll never know real peace until we open up those inner fears to Jesus. We must face them in order to be whole. From that place of wholeness, we are then equipped to convey God's love to the next generation.

God, grant me the courage to face those broken places in my soul, so that I can be strengthened to carry Your love to my children. Thank You for working inside my heart and soul to make me a better father. Amen.

THE STRAIGHT PATH

We must keep our eyes on Jesus,
who leads us and makes our faith complete.
HEBREWS 12:2 CEV

A fresh snow had fallen, and a father decided to go for a walk with his young son. As they hiked along the path, the dad said, "Son, I want to challenge you to a contest." He motioned to a fence about thirty yards away. "See that fence?" he said. "I wonder which one of us can create the straightest line of footprints in the snow from here to the fence. You go first." The boy smiled, relishing the challenge. With great care, he put one foot in front of the other, working diligently to keep the line as straight as possible. After several minutes of concerted effort, he reached the fence and looked back to survey his straight line. To his dismay, the line was not straight at all, but meandering and crooked.

"My turn," the dad said. He strode toward the fence, covering the distance in just a few seconds. The boy was amazed. His dad's path was perfectly straight.

"How did you do it?" he asked.

"Very easy," his father said. "I just picked a post on the fence, and I walked straight to it. I didn't worry about keeping my path straight. Instead, I just kept my eyes on the fence post."

As we teach our sons and daughters to live a good life, there are two ways to approach it. Like the boy, we can focus their attention on their steps, focusing on their actions, trying to keep each step straight. Or, like the dad, we can fix our eyes, our attention, our love, on something else—Jesus. We can inspire our children to love God wholeheartedly. When they do, the path will take care of itself.

God, please enable us as a family to fall in love with You. Please inspire my children to know and value You first and foremost, so that everything else in their lives can fall into place. Amen.

COOLING OFF

"In your anger do not sin."
EPHESIANS 4:26 NIV

A young father labored long and hard, making a
model of an ancient sailing ship. At last, he finished
and put his creation proudly on display. But their
father's masterpiece was not the focus of attention
for his two school-age sons. Instead, they were
quarreling. The older boy shoved the younger.
Furious, the younger son grabbed the TV remote
and hurled it at his older sibling. Big brother ducked.
Mom walked in just as the projectile scored a direct
hit on their father's precious creation, shattering
it into a thousand pieces. There was a long pause,
followed by blame shifting.

"Enough!" Mom said. "Pick up the pieces. Put
them on your father's desk. He will deal with you both
when he gets home."

The brothers' argument was long forgotten by
the time their dad arrived home, replaced by dread
for what he would do. They huddled in their room,
waiting, listening. Supper was eaten in silence. The

boys poked at their favorite meal of macaroni and cheese as if it were boardinghouse gruel. That night and the next day, the boys tiptoed around their dad, but he ignored them. Finally, just before supper, he called them over and said, "When I came home and found that you had destroyed something I had worked so hard to create, I was angry enough to push you or throw something at you. Do you know that?"

"Yes, sir," each boy mumbled.

"But I didn't do that. I gave myself a full day to calm down, so I wouldn't do something to you that I would later regret. Do you think you boys could learn to do the same with each other?" By our actions, we teach our children how to control their anger.

God, when I get angry with my family, please empower me to pause, to cool down, and not to respond in anger. Please give me Your patience and Your self-control in those volatile moments. Amen.

HONEST TO GOD

I cried aloud to the LORD,
and he answered me from his holy hill.
PSALM 3:4 ESV

One of the most important steps in our Christian journey is learning to get real with God. Polite prayers may have their place in polite company, but we don't begin to change and grow in our faith until we start bringing our real thoughts and feelings to God. Do we have doubts? We bring them to God. Do we have fears? We don't deny them; we share them with our Father in heaven. Are we angry? We let God know. Even when we are angry with God—especially if we are angry with God—we don't hide our feelings from Him.

We all experience times in our lives when God does not make sense. He may seem far away. He may seem aloof, uncaring, weak, or cruel. In reality, He is none of those things, but we need reassurance, not at an intellectual level but at a deep-down gut level. We sometimes need to get someplace alone and yell out our frustration, our disappointment, our exasperation with God. But then after we've gotten as honest as we know how with Him, we pause. It's His turn to be honest with us. We let Him—by His Spirit, by His Word, by other people—guide us to the truth we need to enable us to get the fresh perspective that turns everything around.

This is why we take time to listen to our children. This is why we don't shut them down when they share honestly from their hearts, even if we don't like what they're saying. We listen. We let them get real with us. And then, after they know that they've been heard, we find that teachable moment and share with our children what they need to know in order to grow.

God, please enable me to get real with You. Please grant me the grace to allow my children to be honest with me. Give me the power to listen, and help me make the most of my teachable moments with them. Amen.

THINGS TAKE TIME

*Rest in the Lord; wait for Him and
patiently lean yourself upon Him.*
PSALM 37:7 AMP

It costs more than $4 billion—that's billion with
a b—to build a nuclear-powered aircraft carrier. To
create this floating fortress that will travel the seas for
fifty years with only one stop for refueling, to create
four and a half acres of flight deck, to put together a
million-plus different parts and nine hundred miles
of cable, is a big job. Forty million hours of labor go
into its construction. That's the same as one person
working nonstop, around the clock, for 4,566 years.

Some things take time. As men, we understand a
few things about construction. For example, we know
that we can't move into a home on the second day of
construction, because there's nothing to move into.
At best, there's a hole in the ground, and maybe some
wet concrete. No matter how patient or impatient we
are, the job will still take months to complete.

God understands this reality as well. He
understands that it takes time to build a life. Our

children don't grow up overnight. They will spend a lot of time doing the silly, immature things that kids do before they leave that season of life behind and move on to a more grown-up way of approaching things.

That's why, as dads, we relax and enjoy the ride. Yes, we are hard at work helping our children construct a good life. Yes, we do our best to build character and teach important lessons. But when our kids act like kids, we smile and accept them for who they are. As we do, we are reminded that our Father in heaven understands that we are works in progress, and He's okay with that. He empowers us to grow, but He doesn't do the entire job overnight.

God, please help me to be patient with the pace of life. Thank You that I get to have a front-row seat watching my kids grow up. Thank You that You keep working with us without giving up. Amen.

Pray Until Something Happens

Keep on praying and never give up.
LUKE 18:1 CEV

During World War II, a young man felt that God was calling him to be a missionary in China. He spent years studying the language, the history, and the culture in preparation for his life's work. But when the time came to begin, the Cultural Revolution changed everything in China. The borders closed. The practice of Christianity became illegal. Foreign missionaries were executed, imprisoned, or deported.

Everything about it seemed wrong. The young man was sure he had been called to China, but China was no longer a possibility. So he detoured to Korea, and worked as a missionary in South Korea for many years. But he never forgot the Chinese people. Night after night, he prayed for them. Many times he questioned how God could have allowed China to close, but he kept on praying.

Finally, decades later, it became legal to visit China—not as a missionary, but as a tourist. So he made arrangements to visit. As he traveled through this nation that had occupied his attention and his prayers for so many years, he was astounded. Even though he hadn't been allowed to set foot in China as a missionary, God had listened to his prayers and the prayers of many, many other people around the world. The underground Church in China was vibrant and alive. Even though its members were sometimes imprisoned and even tortured, the Church had grown, and multiplied millions were now following Jesus.

Sometimes it seems as if God isn't listening and that the prayers we pray, especially for our children, bounce off the ceiling and go nowhere. But Jesus instructs us to never give up. Remember the acronym PUSH: Pray Until Something Happens. God is listening. He does care. We will see results.

God, empower me to persevere.
When it feels as if my prayers are going nowhere,
please give me the strength and the faith to keep
on praying in a way that pleases You. Amen.

BRINGING CHILDREN TO JESUS

"Let the children come to me, and do not hinder them."
LUKE 18:16 ESV

About two thousand years ago, there was a man who was going through life as a quadriplegic. Life was extraordinarily hard for him and for those who were taking care of him. But he was fortunate to have good friends. One day, his friends learned that Jesus was visiting nearby. So they put the paralyzed man on a stretcher and carried him on foot to the place where Jesus was. But when they got there, there was no way to get close to Him. The crowd overflowed the house, and people were peering in through the doors and windows.

But then the men came up with an idea. Why not climb onto the roof? It didn't get them all the way to Jesus, but it got them closer. They climbed up onto the flat roof, where another idea occurred to them. Perhaps they could remove the roof tiles and at least see Jesus from above. Once the tiles were out of the way, they decided to go the rest of the way. Tying a rope to each corner of the stretcher, they lowered their disabled companion through the roof right down to the floor in front of Jesus. In a few minutes, the paralyzed man could stand. He could walk. He could jump, dance, and run. He was healed.

So much of being a dad is about bringing our children to Jesus. Yes, there will be obstacles, but we keep finding creative ways around them, because connecting our kids with Jesus is everything.

Jesus, most of all I want my children to find You.
I want them to know You, to invite You
into their lives as their Lord and Savior.
Show me how to bring them to You. Amen.

TEACHING CHILDREN TO PRAY

"Lord, teach us to pray, just as
John taught his disciples."
LUKE 11:1 NIV

Relationships require communication. In our
relationship with God, that communication is called
prayer. As fathers, we have the responsibility and the
privilege of leading our children into a relationship
with God that includes meaningful prayer.

One family did it like this: They kept two jars.
When they had a prayer request, they wrote it down
and put it in the jar. Later, when the jar was full, they
started taking out the pieces of paper with the prayer
requests on them. If the request had been answered,
they wrote it down in a journal of answered prayers. If
the request was still pending, they prayed for it again
and put it in the second jar. When the second jar was
filled, they repeated the process.

Of course, prayer is much more than just asking
God for things. That's why we incorporate other
approaches as well. Another way to teach children to
pray is to give them a prayer sentence to complete.

For example, "God, today I feel. . ." or, "God, the thing I am most happy about is. . ." Some dads use prayer acronyms such as ACTS (A for adoration or praising God, C for confession, T for thanksgiving, and S for supplication—that is, asking God for things). The Lord's Prayer found in Matthew 6 is a model prayer—not just a set of words to repeat but an outline to follow. How do we want to see God's name honored? How do we want His will to be done?

The best way to teach our children to pray is to set an example by practicing meaningful daily prayer ourselves. The more we learn to connect with God, the easier it will be to inspire our children to do the same.

*God, please empower me to guide, teach,
and inspire my children to connect with You
in a meaningful way in prayer. Please bring Your
presence and Your wisdom into this process. Amen.*

TEACHING THE BIBLE

*The Bible shows you how to get right with God
and be safe forever. All of it comes
from God and benefits us.*
2 TIMOTHY 3:15–16 TEB

The Bible can have a powerful impact on our
children. A little boy and his dad were having lunch
at a hospital cafeteria on the occasion of the birth
of the boy's baby brother. Evidently, the children's
Bible storybook had made an impression on the
little tyke. Taking his cue from the story of David
and Goliath, the youngster stood up in the booth
and turned around and faced the scores of doctors,
nurses, and visitors. Then, at the top of his lungs, he
bellowed out Goliath's challenge: "Choose a man to
fight me!"

We never know what a child might say. But we
do know that the teachings of the Bible have been
trusted throughout the ages for spiritual guidance.
Unfortunately, many adults find the Bible a difficult,
forbidding book. How can we as dads hope to teach
the Bible to our children?

Reading age-appropriate Bible storybooks to our children when they are young can make the job easier. Of course, we don't stop there. As our children grow, we introduce them to portions of the Bible that will be most relevant and helpful. The more at home we are with the Bible, the more we can help our kids. A number of tools are available for this; an online search will show sites and other resources that make the Bible easy to understand. One dad listens to the Bible on audio as he's falling asleep. He says it helps him understand how the themes and stories in the Bible fit together. Each time we read the Bible with our children, a seed is planted. The harvest is a godly life.

God, please open my eyes when I read the Bible to better understand Your message. Empower me to inspire my children to read and love Your Word. Thank You for the wisdom You have shared with us. Amen.

TOMORROW'S LEADERS

What do you know about tomorrow?
JAMES 4:14 CEV

When Katie Davis graduated from high school, her parents assured her that she could attend the college of her choice. But a different dream had grabbed her attention. Postponing college for a few months, she climbed onto an airplane, crossed the Atlantic Ocean, and settled into a room in a school in a village in the African nation of Uganda. While her parents waited in Brentwood, Tennessee, things were unfolding for Katie much differently than they had imagined. Homeless children were attracted to this young woman. She somehow found food to feed them, medical care to heal them, and money to educate them. Her room gave way to a house. Little girls who had no place to live moved in with her. One day, the unexpected and miraculous happened. A little girl who had no home, other than the one Katie provided, looked up into her eyes and asked, "May I call you Mommy?" And Katie found herself saying, "Yes."

Today, Katie is the mother of thirteen adopted

daughters. She lives with her family in Uganda. The ministry she started is helping to lift thousands of children out of the grip of poverty. Her story has been told and retold around the world through her bestselling book. Her example is inspiring millions of people to reach out and care for the poorest of the poor.

We never know what kind of beautiful future God has locked up inside the children He has put in our care. God-given passions and desires may take our children to destinations we cannot imagine. Children are the future. As dads, we are coaching tomorrow's leaders.

Thank You, God, for the privilege of being a dad. Thank You for the beautiful future You have planned for my children. Empower me to coach them well and release them into Your good hands. Amen.

FINDING THE NEW

Forgetting what is behind and straining
toward what is ahead, I press on.
PHILIPPIANS 3:13–14 NIV

As dads, we are painfully aware of our imperfections. We wince when we think of moments when we lost our temper, failed to keep a promise, or totally misunderstood one of our children. It's easy to be a great dad in theory, but it's a lot harder in real life.

In real life, children get sick. They don't sleep through the night. They whine. They negotiate. They expect their parents to arbitrate squabbles that would give a television-court judge a headache. They step in front of traffic and go wandering off at the mall. They drag home stray animals. They inform us of commitments they've made about five minutes before the family needs to change course in order to keep them. They come up with the wildest needs at the most inappropriate times. All of this conspires to leave us dads sleep-deprived, cranky, clueless, and out of sorts.

Every dad makes mistakes. We fail. We burn

out. We wear out. Sometimes we wimp out. We break down. Our patience wears thin. We are imperfect fathers raising our children in an imperfect world. We deeply want to parent well, to care for these precious lives God has put in our hands. But we know that our children are going to grow up with some ugly memories of dad at his worst.

How do we cope with that reality? Beyond the given—apologizing and seeking to make things right whenever we can—we live in the now. Our focus is not on what we did wrong yesterday, but rather on what we can do right today. It's not maintaining a perfect track record that matters. It's finding and doing the right thing right now that counts. We must seize the opportunities as God gives them to us.

God, please open my eyes to the now. Empower me to see what good I can do right now for my children. Please forgive my wrongs and undo the damage I've done. Let me bring good to my children today. Amen.

HEALING OUR WORLD

*Praise be to the God and Father of our
Lord Jesus Christ, the Father of compassion
and the God of all comfort.*
2 CORINTHIANS 1:3 NIV

We live in a messed-up world, and dysfunctional families are found in every part of it. As dads, we all have moments when we watch other parents bully their children, and we secretly wish we could put that other parent in a time-out chair. (Or maybe we'd like to go a round or two with that dad in the ring!) It is frustrating to watch other people parent poorly. Parental misbehavior can carry a lifelong toll for a child. We all make mistakes, of course, but sometimes the actions of other parents go beyond mistakes. Sometimes it's enough to make us angry. But that anger is all dressed up with no place to go. Outside of those extremely rare occasions when it is necessary to seek legal intervention, there's usually little we can do in the moment to change things. That's tough. No man wants to feel powerless.

But perhaps we're not helpless. Maybe there is

something we can do. Maybe we are growing the antidote for all the venom that is being injected into our world. Among other things, we are raising our children to be healers of the hurt that is felt so deeply by so many. We know that we can all be healers in our own way. Sometimes it's a smile. Or it may be a word of encouragement. Healing might come in the form of friendship or mentoring. Some will raise children who will become professional healers, doctors, nurses, therapists, and counselors. But we all will bring up children who are capable of carrying God's comfort into the lives of hurting people wherever they may be found.

God, let us be a healing family. Empower each of us to bring encouragement, goodwill, and hope to others around us. As a dad, let me be an example to my children in this area. Amen.

A Fresh Start

*The kind of sorrow God wants us to experience
leads us away from sin and results in salvation.
There's no regret for that kind of sorrow.*
2 CORINTHIANS 7:10 NLT

A dad decided to take his youngest son sledding.
He invited the child's mother to come along, but she
refused, rehearsing the dangers of sledding and the
seriousness of broken bones. She preferred to worry
from the comfort of home. But the dad wasn't worried
at all. He dressed his son up in a snowsuit like the kid
from the movie *A Christmas Story*. He thought, What
could possibly go wrong?

The first time down the slope, the sled hit a
bump. Boy and sled separated midair, and the boy
tumbled down the hill, bouncing and rolling, until
he finally came to rest at the bottom. Dad watched
the whole thing in slow-motion horror, imagining his
child unconscious with multiple injuries. The boy lay
there for five long seconds as his father made his way
down the hill, mentally rehearsing what he was going
to say to the 911 dispatcher. But then the child stood

up. He looked back up at his dad and smiled. With bright eyes and a cheerful voice he said one word: "Redo!"

"Redo" has become a motto in that home. When one of the kids rolls his eyes at his mother when she asks him to do something, Dad doesn't say, "Go to your room." He doesn't get angry and launch into a lecture. Instead, he smiles and says, "Redo." This practice helps his kids know that yes, they messed up, but no, it's not the end of the world. They just need to redo.

The reset button for our lives is always available. We all screw up. But we can always turn to God. He is the God of redo, the God of a fresh start.

God, thank You that a fresh start is always only a moment away. As I raise my children, help me to show them that we don't need to get stuck in failure, that success is just a matter of starting over. Amen.

NOW I BELIEVE

Jesus told them, "This is the only work God wants
from you: Believe in the one he has sent."
JOHN 6:29 NLT

Becoming a father can be a spiritually transforming
experience for us. Every dad's journey is different, of
course. One young father had rejected the whole idea
of God, possibly because of his experiences with his
own father growing up. In that case, his father carried
around a laundry list of every time his son had failed.
Whenever the dad was angry, he pulled out the list.
When it came to the son's failures, the dad seemed to
have the memory of an elephant. As he grew older,
the boy decided he didn't want any more of that. In
his mind, he certainly didn't want or need a God in
heaven keeping track of his mistakes and throwing
them in his face every chance He got.

But at 3:30 one morning, his wife woke him up.
Contractions. And they were getting stronger. They
made the drive to the hospital. Hours later, this
adrenaline-pumping but exhausting process was
coming to a conclusion. Finally the doctor motioned

to the young man. "Dad, do you want to hold your child?" As he held his firstborn son in his arms, it slowly began to sink in: *I am responsible for this life.* He was holding eternity in his hands.

This was the beginning of a whole new dimension in his relationship with God. He began to see that God was not the controlling, angry deity he had imagined. Instead, he saw that God loved him unconditionally just like he loved his new son. And so began his journey to faith.

Thank You, God, for what You teach us about Yourself through our experience as dads. Help me to be a good dad to my children so they can see Your heart in my actions. Amen.

HE IS HERE

*God assured us, "I'll never let you down,
never walk off and leave you."*
HEBREWS 13:5 MSG

One of the big challenges of faith is trusting a God who appears to be absent for no reason. Many of us have felt abandoned by God during those times when we needed Him most. We don't understand what He is doing, or why He seems to delay in coming to our aid.

Parenthood gives us a new perspective on this common issue. As fathers, we know that our children don't always have the same information we have. As a result, their perspective gets skewed; they don't see the whole truth.

A young dad and his son shared a unique connection, a strong father-son bond from the moment the boy was born. One night, the dad put his little baby in the crib to sleep. As soon as he left the room, however, the child started crying. The dad walked back over to the crib. Baby stopped crying. He stepped away; his son cried. He came back; the crying stopped. This happened three or four times. Finally the dad said to his son, "Even when you can't see me, I'm still taking care of you."

Just as the words left his mouth, something supernatural happened. For starters, his son calmed down and went to sleep. Dad left, the baby slept, and there were no more problems the rest of the night. But just as important, the father felt that the words he had spoken weren't just for his son. God was speaking to him, as well. He realized that it was God's way of telling him that He was always with him, whether he felt His presence or not. We may not feel like God is there, but He is ever present with us.

Father God, thank You that You are still taking care of us, even when it doesn't seem like You are near. Please assure my family of that truth so we can honor You by trusting in You. Amen.

LEARNING FROM OUR CHILDREN

*The wisdom that comes from heaven is first of all pure;
then peace-loving, considerate, submissive, full of
mercy and good fruit, impartial and sincere.*
JAMES 3:17 NIV

Many times, God can use children to soften the
hearts of their fathers. As dads, we quickly learn that
our children were placed here to teach us, at least as
much as they were put here to learn from us. Being
a dad—especially a dad who cares—is a learning,
growing experience.

Bedtime stories are an important ritual in many
families. A dad who enjoyed making up stories for his
daughters often made the girls the main characters
in those stories. He placed his daughters in a setting
from the time of Jesus, or King David, or another
period in history, and created a narrative that not
only taught facts about history but also conveyed a
moral lesson.

One night, after a particularly rough evening
with his children, the dad sat down in their room and
told a story as usual—even though he was still hurt

and upset by the events that had transpired earlier in the evening. He loved his daughters dearly, but right then he was having trouble liking them. Those emotions played front and center as he told his story. When he finished, one of the girls looked up at him and said, "Dad, that story was about what happened this evening with us, isn't it?" He admitted that it was. Then his daughter stood up, walked over, hugged him, and prayed for him. He wasn't expecting that.

Sometimes, dads need teachable moments, too. That was one for this dad. In his daughters' actions, he felt that God was speaking to him. See their love for you? See how your daughters care about you? That's how I want you to approach them. As dads, we have much wisdom to share with our children. But we must package those lessons with love.

God, please open my eyes to see what
You are teaching me through my children.
Empower me to approach them not only with
Your wisdom but also with Your love. Amen.

TAKE MY CAR

Fathers, do not provoke your children,
lest they become discouraged.
COLOSSIANS 3:21 ESV

A father went through a divorce when his son was young. After custody arrangements were made, the boy became a member of two households with two sets of values. When he started school, he was subjected to yet another set of values. Dad knew that he was competing in some ways for his son's heart, but he always encouraged the boy to show respect for his mom and his teacher, and obey their rules. At the same time, he wanted to build a solid spiritual foundation in his son's life, particularly in those early kindergarten and first-grade years. One day when the dad was reading a Bible story to his son and seeking to underscore the spiritual lesson, the boy said, "My mom and my teacher said I don't have to believe anything."

Dad was taken aback. At first, he didn't know what to say. But then an idea occurred to him. He fished his car keys out of his pocket and handed them to his son. "Here," he said, "go out and take the car for a drive."

Now it was the boy's turn to be surprised. "Dad," he said, "you know I can't drive. I'm not old enough. I don't know how. And my legs aren't long enough to reach the pedals."

"That's right," his father answered. "You're not old enough. That's why God gave me to you, because there are some things that I know that you don't."

When a child is confrontational, it may be a teachable moment in the making. All we need to do is step back and let God enter the conversation and perform the miracles that only He can perform.

God, please open my eyes to see the opportunities in disguise all around me. When conversations in my family have the potential to go badly, please come near and turn them around for good. Amen.

No Defense

*"Don't you understand that I could ask
Father God to put the armies of heaven
at My disposal if I wanted to fight."*
MATTHEW 26:53 TEB

Our experiences as dads can sometimes serve as parables with a deeper meaning. A father was dead tired. His youngest daughter was in bed, but she was miles away from sleep. He was trying to extract himself gracefully by saying all those things fathers say: "Time to go to sleep. No more questions. No more stories." But she wasn't hearing him. Earlier that day, they had been talking about animals and plants. They discussed their natural enemies and how each plant and animal has a means of defense; for example, a cactus has needles and a skunk has a smell. They had talked about tigers and teeth, deer and antlers, chameleons and camouflage. They had pondered how some animals travel in herds or packs to keep themselves safe, whereas some are safer all by themselves, hidden away in the forest. All of this was swimming around in her head, and she needed to talk about it. So she looked her dad in the eye and said, "Daddy, what is the dandelion's defender?"

He was exasperated and wanted to blurt out, "The dandelion has no defender; just go to sleep!" But something stopped him. God was giving him pause. He opened his mouth, and these words came out: "Their defense is producing life. Remember those yellow flowers? Remember how they turn white? Each one of those white puffy pieces is a seed. Each one can make a new dandelion plant. So, no, they don't defend themselves. Instead, they produce life."

What a picture of Jesus Christ! He didn't defend Himself. He could have called an army of angels, but instead He fell into the hands of evil men. But, by falling, He produced life.

Thank You, God, for those moments when You use our children to teach us powerful lessons about life. Thank You, Jesus, for not defending Yourself. Thank You for going to the cross for me. Amen.

MOMENT OF TRUST

*He had us in mind, had settled
on us as the focus of his love.*
EPHESIANS 1:6 MSG

Many people, dads included, secretly feel that
God will never really like them because of the bad
things they have done. We may feel too damaged,
too tainted, too ruined to ever have a chance with
God. For many, unconditional love is such a foreign
concept that it doesn't seem real; it doesn't seem
possible.

After a dad moved into a new apartment
complex, he wanted to be intentional about sharing
God's love with his fellow residents. He hosted
weekly meals and invited his new friends to attend.
One of the families that attended was a young mother
with her two small children—one outgoing and the
other, a toddler, very shy. The shy child clung to her
mother and quickly hid behind her anytime anyone
approached. As the dad sat on the floor playing with
the other kids, he tried to coax her over to join them
but with no success. After several weeks of this,

he had all but given up. But one night her shyness seemed to vanish. With a smile on her face and a light in her eye, she waddled over to him, placed something in his hand, and walked away. He looked down. There in his hand was a freshly used tissue.

He did his best to hide his initial reaction. After all, this little girl had finally opened up to him. Then it occurred to him: This is just like coming to Jesus. What do we have to offer? Nothing but our broken lives and the disgusting failure of our sin. But how does He receive us? With open arms. He never turns us away.

God, thank You that even though You know everything there is to know about me, You still accept me and love me unconditionally. Please empower me to love my children in the same way. Amen.

RELEASING OUR CHILDREN

I know the one in whom I trust, and I am sure that he is able to guard what I have entrusted to him.
2 TIMOTHY 1:12 NLT

Our children belong to God. Most parents know that in an abstract sense, but learning it in any real way seems to take a long time for many. A dad taught his daughter to ride her bike. When she disappeared around the block, he almost had a fit until he realized that the problem wasn't with her. It was with him. She was growing up, and he couldn't stop it. Another dad thought he trusted God until he dropped his first child off at college. As he was driving home, he found himself pulling over to the side of the road to cry.

It is hard to let go. So much of our God-given role is to be our children's protector. But sometimes we cannot protect them. A father watched as nurses wheeled his six-month-old daughter off to surgery. He focused on her trusting eyes looking at him through the bars of the crib. He felt like a monster. He was letting strangers cut into her body with no guarantee that she would live through the experience.

But he had no choice. She needed the operation. He had to open his hands and give her to God.

We do our best to be good fathers to our children. But there are limits to our ability to protect, provide, teach, lead, and love. Fortunately, our heavenly Father has no limits. He knows and loves our children so much more than we do. Though God has given us the privilege of being fathers to our kids, He is their eternal Father, and they are safe with Him. We aren't releasing them to the horrors of this world. We are releasing them to the gentle, loving hands that made them.

God, my children belong to You. They are Yours. It's a journey for me to learn to completely trust You with them. But thank You that You will protect what I put in Your care. Amen.

BACK IN THE GAME

Don't ever be afraid or discouraged!
I am the LORD your God, and I will be
there to help you wherever you go.
JOSHUA 1:9 CEV

For one dad, hunting was his passion. For years, he had hunted deer, bear, elk, turkey, and duck. One day he decided to take his youngest daughter deer hunting for the first time. At the age of thirteen, the experience was all new to her.

Father and daughter were in a blind, when a doe started walking near their location. Being inexperienced, the daughter missed several opportunities for a good shot broadside. Then the doe turned and started walking toward them. She was downwind, so it was only a matter of moments before she would pick up the human scent and run. "This is your last chance with this one, sweetie," the dad whispered. The girl took her best shot but missed a dead-center kill shot. The deer was wounded and took off running, leaving a bloody trail for them to follow.

The daughter was excited. She had taken

down her first deer—a rite of passage. But the more they followed the trail, the more doubtful things looked. After a while, all signs of blood disappeared completely. No deer. They circled around and retraced their steps. No deer. Yes, his daughter had definitely wounded the doe, but finding the wounded animal was not to be. What a huge disappointment! The dad knew his daughter had to be crushed. But as he searched for a way to lift her spirits, she gushed with excitement, "Can we come back tomorrow?"

Life is filled with highs and lows, and sometimes they come right next to each other. All of us get knocked down. What makes the difference is how soon we stand up and get back in the game of life.

God, help us as a family to be resilient. Empower us to persevere. When we are crushed with disappointment, please come and show us the truth so we can get back in the game. Amen.

HOME FROM JAIL

*"Celebrate and be glad. This brother of yours
was dead. And now he is alive again.
He was lost. And now he is found."*
LUKE 15:32 NIrV

It was Christmas morning. As the pastor prepared for
the service, he felt excited about sharing his holiday
message with his congregation. He was wearing his
most festive suit and smiling as he headed out. His
son had left a few minutes earlier, and the pastor
looked forward to meeting up with him at the church.
But as he drove over the crest of a hill, a scene
unfolded before him that he never expected. His
son's car was pulled over, surrounded by four police
cars. His boy was in handcuffs, and the police were
searching his car.

The pastor went to church that Christmas
morning, but his son went to jail. The pastor preached
his sermon as planned, never saying a word to
anyone about what had happened. Later, his son
called from jail, asking his father to bail him out, but
the pastor refused. He was seething with anger.

These thoughts kept going through his mind: *We've given you everything. We sacrificed for you, and you threw it all away!*

Even after a friend bailed the son out of jail, the pastor's anger continued to fester, so much so that he couldn't even look at his son. He fully expected that his wife would share his anger, but that's where he ran into something unexpected. When their son walked in the door, his wife threw her arms around him. "Welcome home, son," she said. In that moment, the pastor understood—for the first time—God's unconditional love for us.

People think of God as the man in the sky who is so angry with us that He doesn't even want to look at us. But that's not His heart. Instead, His arms are open, and He's waiting for the opportunity to say, "Welcome home, son. Welcome home."

Thank You, God, for Your welcoming love for me. Please open my eyes to see my children through Your eyes. Let my children learn unconditional love from me, by the power of Your grace. Amen.

SPACE TO CHOOSE

In your heart you plan your life.
But the LORD decides where your steps will take you.
PROVERBS 16:9 NIrV

We want our kids to do things that are good for them. But too much parental control can suffocate them and push them to rebel later in life. We need to give our children room to make their own choices. For example, a young daughter didn't enjoy math. In the past, her father had tried to convince her to embrace mathematics. "This is something you will want later in life," he kept telling her. But now he gives her more room. "If you want my help," he says, "just let me know." This gives her the freedom to determine if and when she wants help. As a result, she's actually much more open to the help he wants to give.

A young boy was just tall enough to hit his head on the corner of the table. Though tempted to try to protect him, his father didn't rush over to prevent it from happening. Soon the child banged into the table. It hurt. There were tears. For the next several days he had a bump on his head. But by refusing to be overly protective, this dad allowed his son to acquire a basic life skill: look where you're going.

Sometimes God takes His hands off our lives to help us realize our need for Him. We may go our own way and bump our heads on the tables of life. Mistakes like alcoholism and sexual irresponsibility hurt. But sometimes God uses our mistakes to show us what was in front of us all along: we need God. God gives us the space we need to freely choose Him.

God, thank You for giving us room to choose and the freedom to experience the consequences of our decisions. Give me wisdom to give an appropriate amount of freedom to my children. Amen.

STORIES OF TRUTH

Jesus used stories when he spoke to the people. In fact,
he did not tell them anything without using stories.
MATTHEW 13:34 CEV

Sometimes we need to see ourselves and our world
from a new and different perspective. A dad often
told his young children stories at bedtime. Their
favorites were tales about a make-believe family
of orphans called the Forest Children. Night after
night, the four Forest Children experienced one
adventure after another as they traveled through the
woods under the watchful care of the Great Eagle.
They learned how to get along when they wanted to
quarrel. They learned relationship skills by dealing
with the cantankerous twins, Bert and Norbert, who
lived nearby. They laughed at Mr. Slitherslather who
ate nothing but candy.

   The dad told his children these stories for about
two years, until one day his oldest child realized
something: "The Forest Children," she said, "they're
us, aren't they? Gabby, Pinball, D, and Suzie—those
are just other names for us!" She was right, of course.

All along he had been telling them about themselves, trying to help them see their world through a different set of eyes.

Stories are a wonderful way of teaching children, because kids tend to remember the plot and the characters for a long time. Later, when they're ready, they will begin to comprehend and appreciate the lessons behind the stories. It's no surprise that God used parables and simple stories to teach His people. Jesus, the master storyteller, used stories to explain many things, including how faith works, why some people follow God and others don't, and how God feels when people come back to Him.

Why stories? Jesus explained that, as well. Stories are like birthday presents. When the time is right, we can take off the wrapping and discover God's truth inside.

God, thank You for packaging what I need to know in a way that I can remember. Open my eyes at the right time so I can see what I need to see. Empower me to teach my children in ways they will long remember.
Amen.

POWER STRUGGLES

A servant of the Lord must not quarrel
but must be kind to everyone, be able to teach,
and be patient with difficult people.
2 TIMOTHY 2:24 NLT

We can avoid power struggles with our children by not turning everything into a battle. For example, a dad used to insist that his kids eat their vegetables. Then one day he realized that his wife didn't eat vegetables. He was the only one in the house who did. A voice inside seemed to be saying, *Let it go.*

In another instance, the dad's daughter wrote some of her own songs. Anxious to preserve them, he arranged for a recording session in their home. But his daughter refused to cooperate. When the time came for her to sing, she was slouched over. "Stand up and sing," he said to her. But no, she wanted to sing slouched over. This conflict brought the recording session to an end. After that experience, he decided he didn't want to deprive his daughter of the joy of songwriting just because he was focused on preserving her work. The voice inside had said, *Let it go.* So he did.

A boy refused to do his homework. Every night was a power struggle. His dad met with his teachers. He tried every parenting trick he knew, but getting even one math problem done was like pulling teeth. What made it even more frustrating was that his son was a walking encyclopedia. He probably knew more history than his teacher, but he was getting a D-minus in the class. Finally, the dad just let go. A year later, his son was getting almost straight *A's* because he was enrolled in welding, construction, and hands-on courses. Dad realized, *This is a good thing. He knows what he likes.*

Some battles are worth fighting. Some are not. We look to God for the wisdom to tell the difference.

God, please give me wisdom as I deal with my children. Help me to avoid power struggles with them. Let me not battle with them over things that aren't that important. Amen.

A Sense of Wonder

*As the waters fill the sea, the earth will be filled
with an awareness of the glory of the LORD.*
HABAKKUK 2:14 NLT

Often, one of the casualties of growing up is that we
lose our sense of wonder. We become sophisticated,
even jaded. We've seen it all, done it all, and nothing
impresses us anymore. This is a great loss because it
impedes our ability to appreciate God and the beauty
that is so connected with Him.

As dads, we have the great privilege of
rediscovering our world each day through the eyes
of our children. A little baby discovers her fingers
for the first time. A trip to the zoo or the aquarium
becomes a voyage of wonder. Getting stuck waiting
at a railroad crossing becomes an opportunity to play
"Count the Cars."

A dad was at a professional baseball game with
his young son. The boy—apparently a civil engineer
in the making—looked around the covered stadium
and said with excitement, "Dad, this is one big room
made out of metal and concrete!"

What are our children teaching us? They teach us to see the same old things through new eyes. They teach us that a grasshopper is a marvel, blowing bubbles and watching them float away is great fun, and clouds are works of art. They teach us to slow down, to stop and see what we can't see when we're traveling 100 mph through our adult world.

Jesus taught us that to find God we must become like children. No wonder the enemy of our souls works so hard to keep us caught up in the complicated and hurried affairs of life. The eyes of a child help us discover the fingerprints of God in our world.

God, thank You for what You are teaching me through my children. Open my eyes to see what they see. Keep me from being jaded. Restore a sense of wonder inside me so that I can worship You. Amen.

THE PATH TO GROWTH

What right do you have to criticize someone else's servants? Only their Lord can decide if they are doing right, and the Lord will make sure that they do right.
ROMANS 14:4 CEV

For many years, a young boy couldn't read. Though some kids were starting to read at age four, he wasn't interested. Alphabet and phonics lessons at six and seven didn't stick. His dad wasn't overly concerned. Many kids, especially boys, start reading late. The family was homeschooling, so he wasn't at risk for teasing or bullying. The boy's parents didn't make an issue of the boy's late development, until at age eight when the boy brought it up.

Walking through the library in search of some books one day, he said, "Dad, it really bothers me that I can't read." His dad told him the story of Albert Einstein, of how he got a slow start, but that didn't help much. The boy's pain intensified as he got further involved in the kids' program at church. It was workbook intensive, and it was painfully obvious that he was the only one in class who couldn't read a word of it. Every Wednesday night he would get a stomachache and beg to not go.

At age ten, the boy still wasn't recognizing the letters of the alphabet. His dad took him to a specialist for neurological testing. In the midst of that six-month evaluation period, something miraculous happened. Around age eleven, the alphabet started making sense. Phonics started to work for him. By age thirteen, he was reading at grade level. Now he's a college student with an above-average IQ, who reads constantly, illustrating that people master skills at different times and in different ways.

God doesn't pigeonhole people. He lets people grow in different ways. Each person's spiritual journey is unique. Just as this young man learned to read when he was ready to read, so also each person will grow when they're ready.

God, grant me the patience to let my children grow the way they were designed to grow. Allow me to appreciate the diversity of people around me, without trying to squeeze others into the mold of my expectations. Amen.

ETERNALLY RELEVANT

*Jesus Christ is the same yesterday
and today and forever.*
HEBREWS 13:8 NIV

Sitting with a group of teens, one dad noticed
that they were all cradling their phones in their
hands, texting away. "Hey, did you hear," he said
to the group, "they've come out with a new cellular
technology. It's where you use your voice."

"You mean voice to text?" one of the girls asked
him, clearly thinking there was no way this old man
could be more tech savvy than she was.

"Even better," he said with a smile. "Voice to
voice."

She looked at him, confused, for a long moment
and then went back to texting.

There will always be differences between
generations. People who are part of the Baby Boom
generation experienced generational issues with
their parents' generation, the Builders, the people
who survived the Great Depression and World War
II. Builders could never figure out Boomers' endless

obsession with "finding themselves." For most Builders, it never mattered whether a person liked his job or hated it—one should choose the job that paid the most, because that's what work was for: earning money. To Boomers, that was ridiculous. Why would you spend your life doing something that "wasn't you"?

Our children will be children of their generation. They will absorb many of the values, perspectives, and practices of others their own age. That is unavoidable. But it is also an opportunity. We can learn from them. We can encourage them in the strengths of their generation's point of view, and fortify them in those areas where we offer a stronger perspective. Most of all, we can remind our children and ourselves that—regardless of passing fads and customs—our unchanging God remains eternally relevant.

Thank You, God, that You remain the same, yesterday, today, and forever. Please help me see and communicate to my children how relevant You are to every part of our lives. Amen.

STANDING AGAINST THE FOE

Let the Lord make you strong.
Depend on his mighty power.
EPHESIANS 6:10 NIrV

While bow hunting for bear in northern Manitoba, a hunter first encountered "Scarface." While he was working a bait, about ten different bears came and went. But he didn't want just any bear; he wanted a trophy—a twenty-inch skull. Unfortunately, he was shooting video instead of arrows when two boars came through, following a sow in heat. By the time he realized he had just seen a seven-foot black bear, it was too late. The animal was out of range. As the hunt drew to a close, he was forced to settle for a lesser animal. But he had no sooner killed the smaller bear when Scarface, the seven-foot bear, showed up again. Before the man could get to his kill, Scarface grabbed up the smaller animal with his massive jaws and dragged him deep into the undergrowth.

In the gathering darkness, the hunter wondered what he should do. His preferred trophy was right in front of him, but he couldn't shoot it. He had only one tag, and Scarface was busy tearing that bear apart. He had no choice. He had to run him off, but that was easier said than done.

The hunter charged. Scarface retreated then stopped, turned around, and started walking back toward the man. The hunter charged again. Same response. This happened five times before the bear finally backed down and wandered off.

As dads, it's our job to take a stand against everything that would like to tear apart our families. How we do that varies depending on the situation, but God will give us the courage and confidence to prevail.

By the way, the hunter returned to Manitoba every year. Finally, after a couple of years, he tracked down Scarface and shot him. He got his trophy bear.

God, grant me the strength, wisdom, and courage to fight against the things that fight against my family. Thank You for providing the armor and resources I need to prevail. Amen.

A WELL-PLACED SHOT

"Keep us from falling into sin when we are tempted.
Save us from the evil one."
MATTHEW 6:13 NIrV

The German battleship *Bismarck* was the largest battleship in the world in its time. It was nearly three football fields long. The weight of water it displaced was about the same as twenty-five thousand automobiles. It carried eight fifteen-inch guns. These guns could fire a one-ton shell that could travel more than eighteen miles at over 750 mph. Not only powerful but accurate, the ship's targeting system aimed those shells so precisely that the *Bismarck* destroyed the British battle cruiser HMS *Hood*, the pride of the Royal Navy. The resulting explosion was recorded as one of the largest explosions in World War II. In addition, the *Bismarck* was heavily armored, so that even a direct hit by a torpedo would do little damage. This monster ship was the undisputed heavyweight champion of the seas at the beginning of World War II.

Enter Lieutenant Commander John Moffat, a

pilot with the British Royal Navy Fleet Air Arm. Flying a flimsy Fairey Swordfish biplane, he skimmed the waves in the dead of night, in a David-and-Goliath attempt to take on this behemoth. At exactly the right moment, he released a torpedo, which exploded next to the *Bismarck*'s port rudder, locking the rudder in position and making the ship impossible to maneuver. Although the disabled ship remained dangerous, the Royal Navy was able to surround it and finish it off. In May 1941, the *Bismarck* went to the bottom of the ocean, where it remained undisturbed until the wreck was discovered in June 1989 by the same oceanographer responsible for finding the *Titanic*.

Like the *Bismarck*, men and families are sometimes crippled by a well-placed shot. Even the strongest man has vulnerabilities, and a wise dad knows his weaknesses, understands where he can be tempted, and makes provision against it.

God, keep me away from temptations that could harm me or my family. Protect me by Your power. Let me put my confidence not in my own strength but in You. Thank You. Amen.

OVERCOMING DISCOURAGEMENT

No! In all these things we will do even more than win!
We owe it all to Christ, who has loved us.
ROMANS 8:37 NIrV

When our kids experience discouragement, it
can help to ponder what others have overcome.
Beethoven's teacher considered him hopeless as a
composer. Bob Dylan's band lost a high school talent
competition. Thomas Edison's teachers told him he
was "too stupid to learn anything." Albert Einstein
didn't even speak until he was four. His teacher
called him "mentally slow." A movie producer told
actor Harrison Ford that he would probably never
succeed. Henry Ford went out of business three times
before becoming one of the greatest entrepreneurs
in American history. Stephen King threw his first
novel in the trash. *M*A*S*H* was rejected by twenty-
one publishers before becoming a bestselling book,
a huge movie hit, and one of the longest-running
television series of all time.

Douglas MacArthur was twice refused admission
to West Point. He got in on the third try and became

one of the most successful generals of World War II. Marilyn Monroe was told she wasn't pretty or talented enough to be an actress. Babe Ruth held the record for most baseball strikeouts. Before he founded KFC, Colonel Sanders went out of business at an age when most people were retiring. Twenty-seven publishers rejected the first book by Dr. Seuss. Vincent van Gogh sold only one painting in his entire life—not to a customer, but to a friend. Oprah Winfrey lost her job as a television reporter because "she wasn't fit to be on screen."

Our failures don't define us. The opinions of others don't count for much. Only one opinion matters: God's. And He chose us and our children to be part of His family forever. Do we have what it takes? Of course we do. We have the best Dad in the universe, and He is determined to coach us to success.

Thank You, God, for lifting us up when we feel discouraged. Thank You that You have a perfect plan for my children, and You are coaching all of us, empowering us to succeed. Amen.

THINK OUTSIDE THE BOX

"Now I will tell you new things,
secrets you have not yet heard."
ISAIAH 48:6 NLT

Wojtek was probably the most unusual soldier of World War II. Found in Iran by the Polish army when he was young, and adopted by the soldiers after his mother was killed, Wojtek belonged to the 22nd Artillery Supply Company. He quickly grew, and it wasn't long before he was bigger and stronger than anyone else in the unit. In fact, to demonstrate Wojtek's massive strength, five of the strongest soldiers lined up in a tug of war contest against him. With one gentle tug, he pulled all five men to the ground. The soldiers loved Wojtek. He was known throughout the Polish Underground as the "Smiling Warrior."

Wojtek's job was to help carry ammunition to the troops in need. He easily did the work of two or three men. When the unit transferred to Italy aboard a British troop carrier, regulations prevented them from taking Wojtek with them into battle. So the Polish army did what had never been done before. They drafted Wojtek into the army and gave him the rank of private, even though he was less than four years old. By the way, Wojtek was a Syrian brown bear.

As dads, sometimes we need to think outside the box. Each of our children is unique; the mold was broken the moment each one was made. That means each child needs something a little different from us. What works with one, never quite works with another, so no two relationships are the same. We are constantly reinventing ourselves as fathers, adapting to new challenges and opportunities. But that doesn't present a problem, because we are being mentored by a heavenly Father who simply won't fit in a box. His infinite creativity is only a prayer away.

Thank You, God, for sharing this adventure of fatherhood with me. Thank You that You have something new for me every day. Empower me to think outside the box, so I can best care for Your precious children. Amen.

GIVING ALL TO PROVIDE

For God loved the world so much that he gave
his one and only Son, so that everyone who believes
in him will not perish but have eternal life.
JOHN 3:16 NLT

Boxer Billy Miske made his living in the ring. He was good at what he did—almost good enough to be a national champion. In fact, the only losses in his 48-2-2 record were to two champions. One of those losses was to world heavyweight champion Jack Dempsey, considered one of the best boxers of all time.

But Miske carried with him a secret that none of his opponents, none of his promoters—not even his wife—knew. He was terminally ill with kidney disease. His doctor had ordered him to retire from the ring. But times were tough, and his family was depending on him to provide for them financially. So even though he was so sick he could hardly walk, and he couldn't train, he convinced his promoters to schedule a final fight. Amazingly, he not only survived the fight, but he knocked out his young challenger in the fourth round. He took the purse, $2,400, and bought a piano for his wife, toys for his kids, and the furniture he had pawned earlier to survive.

A week later, he was dead at the age of twenty-nine.

Many dads have given everything to provide for their families. They've worked long hours at jobs they hate, often for little pay, enduring abuse at the hands of supervisors and coworkers. Many of these dads do what they do without complaint. It's part of the territory.

Our Father in heaven spent everything He had to provide for His children. He saw that we couldn't provide a way out of our sin and back to Him on our own. He gave what cost Him the most, His only Son, Jesus, to die on the cross on our behalf to provide a way for us to have eternal life.

Thank You, Father in heaven, for giving Your Son to provide a way for us to be forgiven and received into heaven to live forever with You. Jesus, I give my life and my family to You.

TAKING A STAND

*The LORD searches all the earth for people who
have given themselves completely to him.
He wants to make them strong.*
2 CHRONICLES 16:9 NCV

The year 1951 was a magical one for the University
of San Francisco. The school wasn't known for its
football team, but that year the right combination
of talent and coaching came together, and the team
finished the year undefeated with a 9–0–0 record.

Hours after the San Francisco Dons won their
final game, Orange Bowl officials invited the team
to play. It was a dream come true. Playing in a bowl
game would make it much easier for the team's
players to have a shot at a professional career in
football. In addition, the university stood to gain the
financial backing it needed for its struggling football
program.

But 1951 was also the height of the Jim Crow era
in the South. African Americans were not welcome as
equal participants in the white-dominated Southern
culture. The bowl invitation arrived with a condition.

Burl Toler and Ollie Matson, the two black members of the team, were not welcome. Knowing full well what it would cost, every member of the team turned the invitation down. The football program didn't receive the funding it needed, and it never really recovered. But several members of the team went on to play pro football; three members, including Matson, were inducted into football's Hall of Fame. In 2006, surviving members of the 1951 team were at the university's graduation ceremonies receiving honorary doctorates. All three thousand people present rose to their feet to give them a long standing ovation for their act of courage taken fifty-five years earlier.

There will always be forces seeking to sway our children to compromise their values and do something other than the right thing. As dads, we lead the way, teaching our children to stand up for what is right, even when everyone stands against them.

God, please grant my children and me
the courage we need to stand for what is right,
even when our stand is not popular or accepted.
Give us the wisdom to understand the times
and to know which choice is best. Amen.

A NIGHT OF PEACE

While we were God's enemies, he made us his friends.
ROMANS 5:10 NCV

On Christmas Eve 1944, during the Battle of the Bulge, a mother and her twelve-year-old son were preparing a Christmas meal in a small cottage just inside Germany, when a knock came on the door. When the woman answered the door, she was greeted by three American soldiers. They were the enemy, but she noticed that one of them was badly wounded.

"Come in," she said in German. The men were nearly frozen to death. In the confusion of battle, they had become separated from their comrades and had been wandering for three days in the forest. The woman and her son got busy, bandaging wounds and putting together a meal.

Then there came a second knock on the door. This time four soldiers stood there—Germans. Even though the woman knew she could be shot, she told the newcomers they were welcome to spend the night but that she had other guests they would not consider friends. Then, in a firm voice, she told them, "This is

Christmas Eve, and there will be no shooting here." Somehow she convinced all the soldiers to turn their weapons over to her. Then they shared a meal. The German medic aided the wounded American, and all nine people in the house spent the night in peace. In the morning, the soldiers directed one another back to their lines.

Making peace is not always easy, comfortable, or convenient. But, as leaders of our families, sometimes we need to step into explosive situations and act with great courage. The future may depend on our ability to de-escalate conflicts and bring hurt and offended people back into relationship. We take our lead from Jesus, who brought the enemies of God back into relationship with Him.

God, only You can bring lasting peace.
As a dad, I depend on You to bring Your presence
into our family so that hurts can be healed and
differences can be resolved. Empower us as a
family to be instruments of Your peace. Amen.

A Gift from God

Children are a gift from the LORD.
They are a reward from him.
PSALM 127:3 NIrV

It could have been the other way around: our children could have been the parents, and we could have been the children. We could have been born at a later moment in time, and then we would need to answer to our children instead of our children answering to us. We dads know this. Why exactly each of us was given the parents we were given and the children we have is a mystery that we may not fully understand in this life. But we believe we were put here for a reason—in this exact moment in history, in this family, with these children.

We are doing God's work. We are raising His children. No, our children don't belong to us. But yes, we are responsible for them. Parenting is a sacred trust. The moment we become dads, our lives are forever changed. We have taken on a task of eternal significance. We have brought new life into the world, and we have taken on responsibility for nurturing and protecting it.

A newborn baby, a running and laughing child, an ambivalent teen, a young adult testing her wings, the father of our grandchildren, the hands that will close our eyes on this life, the faces we will someday greet from our home in heaven—fatherhood takes us through many seasons, some filled with joy, others riddled with pain.

But we are never alone on this journey. We have a Father in heaven who walks with us as we change diapers, read bedtime stories, wait up past curfew, look for that phone call, offer our parting words of advice. To Him we commit our imperfect efforts to be good fathers to our precious children. In the end, we leave the results with Him.

God, what an honor it is to be a dad to the children You have entrusted to my care. You know that I could never be perfect, but empower me to be the best dad I can be from this day forward. Amen.

SCRIPTURE INDEX